# E-commerce
# Get It Right!

# Welcome to E-commerce Get It Right!

Newly released and written in a no holds barred style... This exclusive step-by-step E-commerce guide with the latest techniques and 10 years of hands-on experience will show you everything you need to know about achieving success with your own e-commerce website and business.

## *Inside You'll Learn...*

- ✓ How to Build & Launch a Super-Charged E-commerce Website & Business – Fast!
- ✓ How to Generate High Quality, Ready-To-Buy Visitors!
- ✓ How to Convert More of these Visitors into Paying Customers!
- ✓ How to Transform a Struggling E-commerce Website!
- ✓ How to Fast Track Your Learning & Avoid the Pitfalls!

## *...and Everything Else In Between for E-commerce Success!*

E-commerce is a booming industry that is growing at a rapid rate and many e-commerce businesses are taking market share from traditional offline retail businesses.

Now is the time to take the opportunity of an accelerated start-up regardless of the economy, your background, age or experience. You'll see how to quickly get accomplished in owning and running your own e-commerce website with E-*commerce Get It Right!*

If you are looking forward to financial independence, moving towards your dream lifestyle, and achieving your career goals, then you have come to the right place.

Within this book, we are going to break down and analyze the four critical steps required to get explosive E-commerce Sales & Profits - within 30 Days of launch and beyond.

We'll cover building your e-commerce success foundation, hiring a kick-ass web designer, how to drive masses of traffic to your website, how to lower bounce and cart abandonment, and how to increase conversion rates, all using simple and common sense yet powerful e-commerce strategies!

## If you're ready... grab your favorite drink and let's get started!

> **Wondering About Your E-commerce Experience Level?** This book is not only for small business start-ups. If you've been trading online with an e-commerce website and are either struggling (as most do - read on for the stats and the solutions!) or just want to increase sales & profits, this book is for you!

# What Do Real E-commerce Website Owners Think of E-commerce Get It Right?

"The *E-commerce Get It Right!* book woke me up to the potential of e-commerce and how successful online businesses operate and can make big profits. It taught me to change the way I viewed e-commerce! As a result my sales increased from 3 to 17 a day within 30 days of reading the book and implementing what's inside." **Paul, In-Car Digital**

"I was able to approach my e-commerce website with a new plan, increasing sales from 1 in 300 visitors-to-buyers to 1 in 75. Using this e-commerce guide gives me new options, and on every page I find gems that I can immediately action on the live website. My advice, read it now." **Steve, Hancocks Jewellers**

"I've been selling online since 2003 on and off of eBay, and I thought I had E-commerce mastery. But using the *E-commerce Get It Right!* book and the techniques, the no-nonsense approach and the practical tips inside opened up a whole new realm of e-commerce profits for my e-commerce websites." **Dean, Funky Footwear**

"My business debts were out of control then a good friend recommended this ebook. Within 2 months I learned how to multiply my web traffic by 3, I increased my conversions by 20% and started to contact my customer database of 20,000 people on a weekly basis. Back-end marketing alone has added at least $2k a month to my bottom-line." **Dan, TGStore.eu**

"What else can I say about *E-commerce Get It Right!* but THANK YOU! Over a period of 2 years I'd used 5 different designers and had a series of poorly designed websites and was tearing my hair out. Not anymore... every designer I work with now has to read it first" **Steffan, Sol-Ace**

# ...And Internet Businesses Who Build E-commerce Websites Daily?

"*E-commerce Get It Right!* helped me refine and enhance customer usability in Etaila software. Ultimately delivering an e-commerce software that looks good, is easy to use, ranks at the top of the search engines and sells products in the thousands per month for happy clients." **Luke, Etaila.com**

"I build e-commerce websites using the Magento open-source platform. Many of my customers have never touched an e-commerce site in their business, but want to take control once its built. I encourage that and as *E-commerce Get It Right!* is an integral part of my package, every customer gets a copy." **Dave, BusyNet UK**

"If you are serious about developing e-commerce websites then *E-commerce Get It Right!* is not only recommended, it's an absolute must. The authors' proven experience in developing, managing and exiting e-commerce businesses gives the reader a great insight and inspiration into what can be achieved. Inside knowledge and practical tips and tricks gives newbies and experienced pros a competitive edge over their competition. I insist all my clients, old and new read *E-commerce Get It Right!* and take their projects to the next level." **Jon, JDCUK.com**

"As a web designer with a graphic designer background I thought I was building stunning websites! I was, and that was the problem: my customers would have a site that was visually stunning, but made few sales. Working with Ian over a 4-year period taught me how to sell online, and enabled me to build sites for my clients that rank high in Google and sell products in bigger numbers." **Andrew, Realtec Media**

"Working with Ian has enabled me to add e-commerce to my CV. His insights, skills and tell-it-like-is style got me from e-commerce zero to e-commerce hero in less than 6 months. My team now builds e-commerce websites and offers private e-commerce consulting for an elite clientele charging from $5K to $25K." **Mike, Synergy Web**

# E-commerce Get It Right!

**Please Note:** I have since sold the websites I once owned used as examples in this book. If you have any e-commerce related questions please email me at info@ecommercegetitright.com and not the websites referenced.

Dedicated to Start-Up and Existing
Online Retailers Across the Globe.

May Your E-commerce Journey Be
Exciting, Fulfilling and Very Profitable!

# Contents

# About This Book

The first in a series of books *'Direct & Simplified'* on the subjects of *E-commerce, Advanced E-commerce & Conversion, Web Business, Web Marketing, SEO (Search Engine Optimization) and Buying and Selling Websites.* They are all taken from over 10 years in the trenches, and real life experience working in these fields with my own e-commerce and website businesses.

The *E-commerce Get It Right! guide* is designed for you to easily and effortlessly assimilate this knowledge. You'll be able to implement the practical tips immediately on your website to maximize sales and profits in the fastest possible time.

The information is presented in a simple-to-use, quick-fire style, with magic bullets one after the other. *For Start-Ups and Websites that are Struggling to make a profit.*

Everything is covered: from planning an e-commerce website and business, to refining and marketing your website to triple or even quadruple sales.

Buying and Selling online is what I do 365 days a year, be it physical products, information products or websites. Most e-commerce websites unfortunately do not survive their first 3 years online so this information is essential for your immediate profitability and long-term e-commerce success.

*Start Up Accelerated With E-commerce Get It Right! Available In Kindle, Paperback, eBook and ePub formats compatible with all eReader devices.*

• *Keep updated on my future books at:* Amazon.com, Kindle Store & IanDaniel.com

'It doesn't matter what product you sell, what country you are based in, or whether you wish to trade locally, nationally or internationally - this book applies to your start-up or your existing e-commerce website and business.'

**Please Note:** All of the information in this book is current and up to date at the time of writing. However, technology evolves fast so look out for my future books on Amazon. com, Kindle Store and other leading online and offline book retailers.

***Coming Soon:*** *Advanced E-commerce Conversion Techniques*

# How to Use This Book

*Choose from 3 Simple Ideas to Help Implement, Maximize and Retain the Information Within:*

1) Simply take notes of important pages pertinent to your website in a word processor such as Microsoft Word, or my recommendation Evernote

2) On a plain piece of paper, draw a line down the middle to make two columns. Top left, write Action Items and top right write Takeaways

   – Action Items: are what you want to implement right now on your website

   – Takeaways: are for your future use and as references

3) Use mind mapping software such as MindManager

   Mind Mapping software lets you create a map with a central topic, and branches connected to this. In the center of the map, write this book & the author's name. On each branch you create, write the book chapter and keywords you are focusing on. An example here might be '*Design Elements*'. Then on each of these branches write the points and references you wish to use and apply now or use later.

---

*Wording Notes:*

   - *Throughout the book, I also refer to E-commerce as Electronic Commerce*

   - *Shopping Cart also means Shopping Basket*

   - *I use Site and Website to mean the same thing*

   - *Web Designer covers Web Developer, Web Agency, and Graphic Designer*

   - *Prospects are Potential Customers before they buy from you*

   - *Stock covers Inventory too*

   - *Shipping is Delivery*

   - *Courier is a Shipping or Logistics Company*

# About Ian Daniel

Thanks for investing in the book! This is NOT another inferior *'written by a ghost-writer'* book rebranded for quick sales. The contents, insights and practical tips inside come from over 10 years online e-commerce experience. I've built up, done business in and subsequently sold 3 e-commerce and information site business networks (total 25 plus sites) all trading profitably. In addition I've built, managed, consulted on and SEO engineered as many websites for happy clients. This is my guarantee to you that you are in good hands.

*Who can best guide you and provide the most effective real life and cutting-edge information for your e-commerce business success?*

1) A web agency who builds websites but has never actually sold a product from an e-commerce website to date?

2) A writer or blogger who writes for a living?

3) Or someone who has built e-commerce websites from the ground up, search engine optimized them to reach top spots in Google, refined them to convert 1 in 33 visitors to a sale (the average is only 0.7 in every 100), sold e-commerce websites for big profit and ultimately lived the e-commerce lifestyle 7 days a week for 10 years?

This book simplifies and demystifies my best ideas, insights and strategies. It also details the mistakes I made so that you can avoid them and get it right from the start. I'm not a professional writer. I've written the book from cover to cover and published the book myself. Refusing to use a fancy-pants writer meant that the book has kept its raw edge - it's important that you feel my enthusiasm. The language may not be the prettiest, but the content is GOLD!

- *Follow my new blog:* www.IanDaniel.com

*'To back up the words within, and guarantee this book you can contact me <u>for free</u> at anytime with your e-commerce questions at info@ecommercegetitright.com... I'm here to help'*

# Introduction to E-commerce Business

## What Is E-commerce?

The Dictionary says: *"e-commerce: Commerce transacted electronically, as over the Internet."*

Synonyms include: *e-commerce, electronic Commerce, E-commerce, ecommerce, online retail, online trading, and selling online.*

Selling and transacting like this can be done thanks to the World Wide Web, which is the global combination of links, information, web pages and e-commerce websites. All of this is delivered to us via the Internet, an infrastructure of computers all linked together.

E-commerce embodies anything from selling a domain name to selling music downloads, or from information products like this eBook to physical products such as a DVD or clothing. Once ordered these products are shipped direct to your customers' door. The term e-commerce is also commonly used for selling physical products to retail customers (Business to Consumer, B2C) and business customers (Business-to-Business, B2B). Therefore, we will focus on these in this book.

## Online E-commerce Business vs. Offline Business.

The advantage of an online business is that you can sell a complete selection of products, with no limits on space. A bookstore can only hold so many books, but online you can display and sell the entire range of book titles the world over, should you wish.

An online business typically has highly automated and more efficient software and systems. Online marketing is highly targeted and ultimately e-commerce overhead costs are lower. On the flip side, if not managed well e-commerce costs can skyrocket and sink your business.

E-commerce businesses do not have a typical storefront with passing trade (footfall), so you cannot be passive and wait for customers to come to you, as many offline retailers do.

However, just like an offline business, a website needs traffic (customers), conversions (sales) and it's essential you build a relationship by communicating with your customers to offer them valuable information and products on the back-end (after the sale is made).

Its important to look at your e-commerce website like a physical store. What I mean by this is; always think about shops you like to buy from when working on the design, adding features, improving usability and especially how products are displayed. Get your customers in with the least resistance as possible and get that sale!

Just like any business, if you do not plan, forecast, budget and do not invest appropriately from the start, you will struggle to make profits and ultimately fail. Be prepared to allocate and invest accordingly into your e-commerce business, website and marketing from the day you start—this means start assertively, not passively!

If you already have an offline business, bolting on an e-commerce business could be the way to double or even triple your profits and reach customers in parts of the world you never knew existed. However, an analysis of the pros and cons must be completed. If approached without planning or checking the numbers it may just add unnecessary costs, which ultimately reduce your profits.

## A Sad Statistic.

Did you know... 97% of e-commerce websites make $0 profits in their first 3 years online. Such is the steep learning curve and skill set required to build an e-commerce website in order to ultimately dominate your product category, market or niche.

Have you heard the phrase *'work on your business and not in your business'*? Well, the 97% referred to above are doing the latter.

> *'Spend 20% of Your Time on Operations and 80% on Marketing'*

Once trapped running your e-commerce website, it's damned hard to escape and spend time where you should be, marketing your business to greater profits. Aim to be part of the profitable 3% as quickly as possible, and your e-commerce sales and profits will skyrocket...

Having been part of the 97% from 2000–03 and subsequently part of the elite 3% from 2004 on doing sales in the multi-millions and growing—in very competitive markets— I can give you the benefit of impartial views and experiences, and I have the *'e-commerce stripes'* to help you.

So it's not all doom and gloom. E-commerce can be exciting, fulfilling and very profitable if you plan from the ground up, grow consistently and get it right from day one. *I'll show you how in this book.*

# E-commerce Success Story.

Amazon.com is the most successful e-commerce website online. It's also my all-time favorite e-commerce website! In 1996 Amazon exploded onto the e-commerce scene pioneering the way in online retailing to date. By February 2010 it had 124 million customers worldwide.

Many companies have tried to imitate but very few can replicate such massive success. Amazon's web team fully understands its web customers, and why they buy from its website.

## Personalization.

Amazon takes marketing to the next level where most websites simply do not. The people at Amazon analyze user data and utilize this to build, design, personalize and structure their website accordingly, to answer their customers' questions, fears and frustrations and match the wants and desires of their customers exactly. They introduced and pioneered product 'Recommendation Engines and Systems'.

This essentially means once you have user data you can target and match your products to your customers' buying interests and behaviors. This then means they SPEND like crazy with you. More on this strategy in Step 2 & Step 4 of the book.

# Thirteen Common E-commerce Mistakes

Let's start by looking at the most common mistakes made by e-commerce websites and e-commerce businesses and why they fail. Read the quick guide below as your first step to avoid falling into the same traps. We'll delve deeper into each point in subsequent areas of the book...

### 1) You Don't Have to Get It Right, You Just Have to Get It Going.

This is critical for an online activity as the internet and technology changes so fast. Too many businesses waste time analyzing, planning and thinking without taking action. These three areas are obviously important, however as soon as the Research, Numbers and Exit Strategy (or goal) is established and make financial sense, then get started. The perfect time will never come, so take action now.

When building a new website, I always push to get it live within 7 days from the date the development starts. This enables me to test the website in a live working environment. Google's spiders can start to index my site immediately, setting me up with an assertive approach and on the front foot. Because customers won't be on the website yet, it doesn't matter if it is not complete.

### 2) Poor Planning, Forecasting & Accounts.

Planning is essential to establish that your new e-commerce website can and will make money. You need to find out:

- If there is a demand for your product online?

- Are the products you intend to sell actually selling online and in what numbers?

- What are your competitors' prices like? Are they charging less than you can buy the product for at trade price? This can happen online

- Will your e-commerce website be profitable?

When your site is trading you must monitor key accounting areas at least weekly - especially your sales and costs, and the resulting net profit (bottom line).

### 3) Trying to Be All Things to All People.

Once you have completed your research, decide on the number of products you will sell a few products, a hundred products or thousands of products? It's your decision, but weigh up the time you have to Source products, Stock products, Sell products, Ship products and Support products. On top of this allow for the time you have to add the products to the website, process orders and do the accounts.

The more pages on a website, the better for SEO (Search Engine Optimization) reasons. However, many product pages will mean you need to do lots of product management. So be honest with yourself before you begin this project and determine if you can actually afford the time spent on the above processes.

You could even split your products into separate websites for each niche or main product category. This would focus your positioning and optimization for each specific product range. Customers will consider you an expert if they see you specializing in one product range. *More on this in Step 1.*

Customer sales usually also means customer support. Over time, you will find and set your own boundaries and limits concerning customer demands and requests. Stick to your principles and run a tight ship. Offer value for money in your business transactions, but do not become a slave to your customers or suppliers. You are in business to make money, not to make friends with everyone, and to provide exceptional '*value-for-money*'.

### 4) Poor Quality E-commerce Software.

Using poor quality e-commerce software will affect usability for you and for your customer. Problems include; a slow load time in your user's browser, poorly laid out products, inferior search engine optimization features, all leading ultimately to an arduous e-commerce experience.

Good e-commerce software loads fast, has a great structure for the user so they can find products easily, and is built so Google can find and index your products with ease.

Flexible e-commerce software that can grow and adapt with your business is essential to automate laborious processes. This will free you up to **work on your business** and **avoid working in it** as previously mentioned.

### 5) Poor Design.

Design is the first visual element that new and existing customers notice on your website when they enter your site. As these processes are subconscious—and adding to the challenge, you only have approx 5–7 seconds to capture your visitor's attention— your design has to be right or your visitor will leave, also known as bounce. Bounce Rate is an online measurement that expresses the percentage of visitors who only see a single page on your website before leaving.

This all starts with hiring the right web designer for your project needs. Most designers simply do not have the innate ability to design good websites, which is why so many websites die a slow death in cyberspace. *You will learn how to hire a great designer in Step 3.*

Avoid using Flash (a tool for presenting images and text in a graphical format) if it is not required. Flash has no place on an e-commerce website as it's big, clumsy, loads slowly and can't be indexed by Google. This in turn means it is bad for SEO. Flash shows off the design skills of the Flash designer but is next to useless when designing a site for profits. There is one exception to this comment: product demo videos produced in Flash can be very useful, but ensure they are compressed using FLV format, so they are quick to load.

Ultimately, your website has to load **Fast**, be **Functional** and be **Familiar**; this is the **3 F Strategy**. Keep the colors clean and pertinent to your positioning and product ranges, and use clean uncluttered text and font styles. Make it easy to read by using lots of background white space, with text headers and items grouped in small boxes or small sizes for quick page scanning.

## 6) *Poor Usability & Conversion.*

Less than one person in every 100 visitors to the average e-commerce website will buy! Increasing this visitor-to-sale conversion rate is all about usability and a simple conversion path. This includes everything from the way the graphics, images, text, navigation menus are used on the website. Prospects (potential customers) need a simple, clean path from entry (entering your website) to exit (having bought your product) without resistance or site elements that make them have to think or work out what to do.

## 7) *Too Busy & Cluttered.*

How many websites have you visited where they hit you with too much content too soon, whether it's graphics, images and options, and where you have no idea where to start? There is no clear entry to the products, no sales funnel, and no clear path through to the checkout. This equals failure!

So keep your design clean and clear, keep it simple, keep it direct and to the point, and give your site visitors what they want in an organized layout from the second they enter to the second they leave. This is about guiding them through your sales funnel.

## 8) *Poor Keyword/Key Phrase Selection.*

Many websites fail to match their site content with the search terms that their prospects search for in Google. This critical component to driving lots of free organic—also known as natural—search engine traffic to your website starts with detailed Keyword research.

When writing content for your website, especially on your home page, category and product pages, you need to target these specific keywords and key phrases—which your prospect will type in the Google search box—in order to get this traffic on to your website.

### 9) Poor Content.

The use of poor content including headlines, product descriptions, font styles, colors, etc., on a website can massively reduce sales. Incorrect spelling (typos), poor grammar, uninspired and feature focused product descriptions all written in a boring style determine whether a customer stays (sticks) or leaves your website. You have approximately 5–7 seconds (maximum) to capture your prospect's attention, when they enter any page of your website. So make your web pages sticky.

Your content needs to captivate, educate and inspire your prospects to want to take action and buy your products, read your blog or sign up to your email newsletter. Use emotional triggers by focusing on benefits, experiences and results that your products will give your prospects and future customers. User Generated Content ads variety.

### 10) Zero or Poor Quality Traffic.

Traffic simply means visitors to your website. Low traffic or traffic that is not targeted to your products will result in zero or poor sales. This is one of the main reasons that so many websites fail. Starting with the right e-commerce software, good design, a strong on-site (also known as on-page) and an explosive off-site (off-page) SEO strategy will give you a solid foundation for e-commerce success. Add the back-end customer communication strategy for your site, and your success is guaranteed.

### 11) Not Analyzing User Data & Testing.

The internet, user behavior and buying habits are in constant change. Most websites owners do not use the free—and very detailed—statistics available to analyze their customer behavior, preferences and the products they buy. Using this free data such as your e-commerce admin statistics, your server logs (hosting account stats) and Google Analytics will present you with key information enabling you to refine your website, resulting in a big increase in sales and profits.

Successful websites including Amazon.com often run multiple tests on their website daily to gather data and respond to the results. They test everything from a simple image placement on their homepage, product layout, Add to Cart buttons, to the messages and products you see when you have placed an order—the order confirmation page.

Further to this, testing allows you to see which areas of your website are performing or where the leaks are that need repairing. When you make changes, ask your family, friends or colleagues to see if your site and its functions are seamless and easy to order. The less experienced the tester, the better, as you will get a realistic view from their responses.

## 12) Unaware of the 80/20 Rule (Pareto's Principle).

Give or take, most web actions and results work out at 80/20 and this simply means 80% of your results (effects) will come from 20% of your actions, products or processes (causes).

As an example, you will find approximately 80% of your sales come from 20% of your product range and 80% of customer service issues will come from 20% of your products. This rule will apply to many areas of your e-commerce business.

Once you have data to work with you can start a '*Best Sellers*' page and promote your top sellers. You can automate and extract your top selling products and display these on the live site. Apply this where you can throughout your e-commerce business and it will help efficiency, productivity, sales and profits.

## 13) No Back-End Marketing.

The majority of website owners—including most e-commerce websites—do not know how, or just cannot be bothered to contact their prospects, once they are sold a product and become customers. Big Mistake! Once you have customers, it's essential to communicate with them regularly via email newsletters, RSS, social and video sites or by traditional mail and offer them more products. Because you have now built a relationship with them—and they have your trust and experience— they are more likely to buy from you, again and again.

*We Have Now Touched On the Negatives & Positives of E-commerce. Your Choice Is: Be Part of the Average, Unprofitable 97%; or Be In the Elite 3% and Be Profitable. So, That Said, Let's Jump Right In With 4 Key E-commerce Foundational Principles...*

# E-commerce Foundation

## 4 Key Principles for E-commerce Success!

→ Discover the 4 Steps to Rapid E-commerce Sales & Profits!

→ Use the Foundational Four to Target High Quality Customers!

→ How the 3F's Will Set Your Site Up for Success!

→ Positioning Your Business!

→ Choosing a Product Category!

→ Become the Leading Voice In Your Market or Crash!

→ Why Problems Are Good & Solutions Are Great!

*E-commerce success comes down to a basic philosophy, can-do attitude and a formula that when planned and executed equals sales, profit and wealth for you and your business. The formula detailed in this book is split into 4 main parts; it's essentially a 4 step Formula with key components described in each of the 4 steps.*

# E-commerce Foundation Principles

Before we get into the four main steps of the book, I just want to touch on the following four simple, yet explosively powerful and essential foundational strategies for any e-commerce website—I call these the **Foundational 4.**

**These are the basic principles that you need to apply, even before we get to the detail in the other** '*Four Main Steps*' that come afterwards in this book.

## *Principle #1)* Traffic > Conversion > Relationships.

### Traffic.

Your website needs traffic. Without targeted traffic your site will get lost in cyber-space gathering virtual cobwebs! Sure, over time, someone will stumble on your website. Some visitors may even buy your product or service, or subscribe to your email newsletter list or blog; however, the numbers will be pitiful.

### *How Do We Get Traffic and Thousands of Visitors Per Month?*

### Strategy.

Because the majority of web searchers use the Google search engine (approx 80%), it has the market share majority with regards to web traffic. The sole purpose of the Google search engine is to send these web users to appropriate and matching sites. This is where your site needs to be. Being in the top 10 is vital - anything under this and your traffic potential plummets. So build your website so that it's Google Friendly!

There are many other different ways to get hordes of ready-to-buy traffic to your new site such as Pay Per Click advertising or social media marketing. However, it makes sense to start with strong foundations and a long term free (organic) search engine traffic strategy in mind.

### Conversion.

Once you get traffic (visitors) to your website, you have to do something with them. Are they taking action? Are you converting them, monetizing them, getting them to subscribe to your email list or selling them your products?

**What Is Your Call to Action or Most Wanted Response?** Let's be clear - with an e-commerce website, you want the sale! As a minimum, you need to capture their email address or get them to click your Adsense advert (publicity that you can put on your site to make you money) when they leave your site—this is a '*monetized*' exit click.

Average conversion rates in e-commerce suck. Approximately 0.7 out of every 100 visitors will buy your product. Your website must have clear text, images, navigation, a clean design and a simple call to action '*Add to Cart*' or '*Add to Basket*'. Visitors must easily understand what you want them to do. If not, forget it – just one '*CLICK*' and they are gone to your competitors!

## Strategy.

A clean, simple yet professional site design, based on a fast, functional and familiar layout. Navigation and structure with clear instructions and content. These are the things to help you to increase your desired conversion rate - anywhere from 1% to 4% overnight. Do the math - if you've been selling one product per day at $100, then overnight after making some subtle design, navigational and conversion changes you could increase this to $400, without spending a cent more on marketing.

With your conversion strategy, you need to take your site visitors by the hand from site entry to exit (with a sale) in as few steps as possible and as fast as possible, with as little resistance as possible.

Resistance can come from many areas such as poor design, poor content and poor navigation, in addition to poor product descriptions and common issues of poor trust and negative security. There are many other areas of resistance that can also hurt success, such as your checkout process, which we will look at later in Step 2.

## Relationships.

This is not an essential component to making a sale (on the front-end) or making an e-commerce site work in the short term. However, Statistics suggest up to 35% of customers will buy from you again if you offer them a further product—once they have already ordered from you. It is obvious that this simple strategy alone could supercharge your profits. This is **back-end marketing.**

Building relationships or communicating is all about providing your visitors with good, useful, reliable content, advice, information and tips and tricks, and of course, product offers mixed in. You can even personalize your emails to match your customers' buying habits by adding their name into the email and promoting products based on their buying history. This is **personalization**.

## Strategy.

After a sale or after subscription to your opt-in email newsletter list or RSS feed, it is imperative to communicate with your customers and communicate often. However, if you only provide low quality regurgitated content or attempts to sell your product or service too hard, one simple click of the 'unsubscribe' link in your email, and your customers could be gone forever.

So, talk to your customers. Offer a newsletter, an RSS news feed, ask them questions via surveys. Run competitions, get them to follow you on Facebook, Google+ and Twitter and give away freebies. Your customers will see you as an expert in your product category, market or niche and will hang on every word you say, resulting in more sales!

# *Principle #2*) 3 F Strategy.

The days of having a simple 5-page brochure website with your company details and a few pictures are long gone. E-commerce websites now generally have at least thirty pages plus, many over a thousand pages. These are big websites with lots of content and multiple images per page.

Yet, a surprisingly large number of businesses both large and small simply do not understand e-commerce. They launch websites that actually drive customers away because they are slow, cluttered and use complex navigational menus that you would need a university degree to understand.

However, you can easily make your e-commerce website work exceptionally well. In fact, the most simple, basic strategies are often the most effective, but the most overlooked. Many of the latest software, web tools and e-commerce modules available offer make it easy for your site to be dynamic and interactive. They allow you to add more content, more easily, without having to call your web developer every time you need to make a simple tweak to the information on your site.

> **'At a Fundamental Level You Need to Implement a 3 F Strategy: Your E-commerce Website Must Be Fast, Functional and Familiar!'**

Most people go onto an e-commerce site with a specific goal in mind - for example buy an MP3 player, DVD or item of clothing. You have to help them accomplish that goal, and fast. People do not want to wait forever to negotiate their way through arty graphics or unfamiliar navigational menus or even worse, wait for Flash to load.

Many sites still have not taken this lesson on board; even a decade after some big name online retailers went belly up. Pretty but ineffective websites with unnecessary Flash interfaces and areas that users never venture into are very common. In addition, even with broadband internet in millions of homes around the globe, many websites still take forever to download. Let's say it again - you only have approximately 5–7 seconds to make them stick, or your prospects are gone!

> **'User Experience and Interactivity Is Critical for Your Success On the Web, As That's All There Is! This Is the Conversion Process Personified!'**

Your site should also function like other successful sites. Therefore, if you design a new menu interface with buttons in unfamiliar places, your users may not know how, or simply not bother to learn how to use it and then leave your site. A user may admire a pretty site once, but they will not return nor make a purchase. In contrast, people will return to a 3 F site ('*Fast, Functional and Familiar*') repeatedly. Your 3 F site will generate sales, repeat traffic and increasing profits.

**Word of Warning:** The danger of the readily available and open source website features and modules is that they have in some instances brought needless complexity within the reach of anyone. This can result in the temptation to spend a lot of time adding them to your site, leading to a huge waste of time, energy and money.

> **'As the Saying Goes: KISS = Keep It Super Simple!'**

## Let's Look Closer At the 3 F Strategy:

### Fast.

This aspect is so important because you need speed in all areas of your business, not just your site in order to succeed. Customers have so many different options online, so why would they wait on you? This encompasses your hosting, site load speed, email responses and your website ordering and checkout process. Just as an example, if your site is slow to load, a customer will more often than not leave right away.

#### Use These Site Components:
- Fast & Reliable Hosting
- Fast Site Load Speed (Maximum 5 seconds per page)
- Compressed & Fast Images
- Fast and Efficient Ordering
- Fast Checkout with as Few Steps as Possible
- Fast Security (SSL Certificate)

## Functional.

Decide from day one, what the goal and desired outcome of your website is. When your potential customers visit your site, can they find a product that they were looking for right away with as little hassle and clicks as possible? Customers are simply going to look elsewhere if it is difficult to purchase products from you! Take the time to think like your customer and complete all of the steps in finding a product on your site and placing an order. Was it easy, does it make sense and would you want to do it again?

*Load Your Website with Useful Functional Features:*

- Use clean, easy to read text, graphics, and navigational buttons
- Make it easy to use and navigate
- Use common features making your visitors' experience helpful
- Give customers what they want in as few clicks as possible

## Familiar.

It is important for customers to feel comfortable on your website, which has everything to do with your chosen layout, structure and usability. For instance if you use strange navigational methods, if it is incredibly difficult for a customer to search for products, find products and buy products, then they will leave your site as quickly as they can click the *'back'* button in their browser.

*You Need to Have Clear and User-Friendly Site Elements:*

- Clear Layout & Structure
- Common Navigation Bar & Obvious Buttons
- Left Product Menu
- Header & Footer
- Clear Text with Headlines & Sub Headlines for Easy Scanning
- Display Trusted Brands & Logos
- Display Accreditations, Card & Security Logos to Establish Trust

## Flexibility & Growth.

Ultimately, you need to decide what your objectives are. Be flexible and don't get too carried away with web-specific ambitions. You do not have to use software that is very expensive and complex; use things that mesh closely with your business's objectives instead. Then get an e-commerce website out there and add functionality, as users demand it. You will never get your site perfect from day one, so test and modify as you grow.

# *Principle #3)* Positioning.

Positioning is about perception and how you want your e-commerce site and business as a whole to be perceived by your prospects and customers. Remember, prospects are potential customers. So ask yourself, do your target customers feel that this is the website they would like to buy from? Position your e-commerce website to match your prospects' ideals.

## Become Your Customer.

Get inside your customers' minds and be them. See, think and feel what they do when buying your product. It is about how your website should look based on its theme, colors, design, layout and branding to make your buyers want to spend time and money there. Essentially, you want something that is contemporary, clean, and inviting to your potential and target customers; often neutral is best with lots of background white space, a clean color, like a light gray and 1 or 2 accent colors to give identity.

As an example, a website aimed at new mothers could use light blues, pinks and images of attractive babies. A website aimed at selling high-end, exclusive furniture might well use blacks, grays and white to demonstrate class, with guarantees and security logos to build trust and show that the website offers customers military strength security and that they are safe to spend here. In either case, use words and language that your target customer understands and uses.

Taking the time to fully understand your target customer will consequently dictate the look and feel of your site, especially relating to the features, layout, design, logo, colors and language used.

## Create & Dominate Your Category.

To become a leading e-commerce retailer in your chosen product area, it is critical you are seen as a leader, a voice that people recognize and trust, and are happy to buy from. This links in with branding, but takes it to a higher level in a number of ways. You'll see this with the big elite companies such as Amazon, Apple and eBay.

### *So Decide Now If You Are...*

1) Entering a small, restricted niche market and selling for example, one trendy brand of women's T-shirts?

2) Alternatively, are you entering a larger niche and selling many brands of T-shirts within the bigger category of clothing?

3) Alternatively, are you entering the top category and selling a large range of clothing and many brands?

This is just a very simple example to detail the different levels. Option 2 above seems to be the more profitable route for small to medium sized businesses to dominate that space. If you go too *'niche'* as in option 1) you can restrict your sales potential, as the market may be very small.

To take this one step further, can you create your own category or niche? Let us say you started manufacturing and supplying your own T-shirts made from a new Eco Friendly material and you called these *'Eco-Tee'* or whatever. This is now a new category—Eco Friendly T-shirts—and you have now just become the expert in this new category.

## Control.

As a website owner you will publish lots of information including product descriptions, how-to guides, blogs, videos, newsletters and RSS feeds. Therefore, through your content make it your objective to control your prospects and customers, and only give them access to the information you feel is right for them, in order to get them to buy your products. This is not about crossing ethical and moral boundaries but essentially leading and directing your product category, market or niche.

This control allows you to captivate, educate, inspire and prime your audience, persuading them that you have a product that fits their needs and wants. This is all about positioning and using psychology or *'mind control marketing'* as Mark Joyner calls it—here is why this is important...

> *'Your Customers Want What You Are Offering, So Do Everything You Can to Give It to Them... Before Your Competitors Do!'*

## Elites & Hierarchies.

When Tim Berners-Lee invented the World Wide Web, his idea was to create a space without rules and regulations that would be equal for everyone including e-commerce entrepreneurs. However, the opposite is happening and those with the biggest resources or category dominance are shouting the loudest and consequently making the most money.

*Let Me Ask You Three Simple Questions...*

1) When you think of a search engine, who do you think of? Google!

2) When you think of buying online? It's Amazon and eBay!

3) When you think of a social media sites? Facebook & Twitter!

However if I ask you about Men's Dating, who do you think of? How about Anxiety Cure? In addition to the big boys like Amazon and eBay, the internet medium has allowed *Double Your Dating* and *The Linden Method* respectively to create and dominate these new information and e-commerce categories. These are just two multimillion dollar and very successful companies from the thousands of new categories being created online. Whether you sell physical products, information products or both, e-commerce is the transaction model used.

So how can you become number one in your category or niche and what will set you apart with your positioning?

## *Principle #4*) **Problem Solution Model.**

Think of the main objective of your website. This is where you get specific and focus on the products and services you are selling to the customer. This is about your web design, text and product descriptions. How they answer a question, a fear or a frustration, and offer a solution to a problem your prospect has. This isn't just about marketing using scarcity as an emotional trigger. It's about taking it to a deeper level mentally, emotionally and spiritually using emotional drivers in your words, images, marketing and website positioning.

It is essential to decide what role your customers' positive and negative emotions will play when they visit your website and want to buy. *You absolutely want to evoke strong positive (they'll feel good if they buy) and negative (they'll feel bad if they don't) emotions by detailing experiences and results to generate an immediate buying response.*

When your potential customer visits your site, they need to find something they can identify with and that will benefit them, remove a problem and offer a solution. You have doubtless heard the saying *'What's in it for me.'* **It's very simple** - that is **all** your customer cares about. What will the product they are buying give them and get them?

If you are promoting a health or weight loss product as an e-commerce store owner, you need to hammer home the negatives (problem) and then offer benefits (solution) your product will give them. It is a great strategy to base the benefits of your product around the current negative situation (problem) your potential customer can identify with, and make the results easy to attain.

***A Few Simple Examples Are:***

- Lose 20 Pounds in 20 Days!
- Discover the Top 5 Secrets to Staying Slim!
- Fast Effective Natural Slimming Aid Accelerates Weight Loss!
- Get back to the Dress Size You Wore in your Twenties!
- Lose Weight The Easy Way!

You need to position and present your website in a way that your potential customers see an immediate benefit for them, so they will be eager to buy and experience the positive result and emotions you are promising. **What is your product going to give to them? What will they get from using and owning your product?** These are critically important things to think about because *that is what your customer will be thinking, feeling and asking...*

***With the 4 Foundational Principles Nailed Let's Start Building Your E-commerce Success Roadmap With Step 1!***

# Step 1—
# Get Started

**Setting Up Your E-commerce Success Formula!**

→ **Discover the Key Steps to Rapid E-commerce Sales & Profits!**

→ **How to Plan for E-commerce Success!**

→ **Use the Foundational Four to Target High Quality Customers!**

→ **Establish Your Goal & Exit Strategy!**

→ **Top 10 E-commerce Project Preparation Essentials!**

→ **Calculating Customer Lifetime Value!**

→ **How to Select the Right E-commerce Software Solution!**

→ **How and Why to Plan, Budget & Forecast!**

# Ten E-commerce Project Preparation Essentials

Now that we've looked at the formula fundamentals for creating your new site strategy with a bird's eye view, it's time to look in detail at the essential and specific components in preparation for a successful e-commerce website.

## 1) Plan for Profit.

This is critical for a successful e-commerce compass and gives you the true picture of where you are before you start and as you progress. They detail your growth or your decline and failings. Numbers do not lie, period!

### Analysis.

This is a time to be realistic and look at your business idea with honesty. Many small business owners try to do everything themselves and 12 months down the line, they realize they are running out of steam—and cash. **So ask yourself:**

- Will your idea work and can it work based on the following points?
- Do you have the resources and money to make it work?
- In addition, do you have the work force to make it happen and will it be profitable?

### Plan.

Your plan will include a small written document covering key areas of your website and business and will keep you focused and on track. You have heard the old adage *'If you Fail to Plan, you Plan to Fail'.* How true - unless you hit the lottery and by pure chance you get it right first time without planning. There is a better way. Stephen Pierce says to be successful you need to be:

## 'FOCUSED. CONSISTENT. PATIENT'

### Planning Software.

You can plan on paper, in Microsoft Word or Visio, or using Mind Mapping software such as MindManager. Your plan does not have to be 100 pages long. Remember KISS? So **Keep it Simple**. Just cover the main areas and use bullets in your Word document or branches in your Mind Mapping software. The most important software for your plan is a spreadsheet, using Microsoft Excel, Google Docs or OpenOffice to handle the numbers and financial forecasting.

### Forecast & Planning Software:

- Microsoft Office: Excel, Word, Visio: www.microsoft.com
- Google Docs: www.docs.google.com
- OpenOffice: www.openoffice.org
- MindManager: www.mindjet.com
- EverNote: www.evernote.com

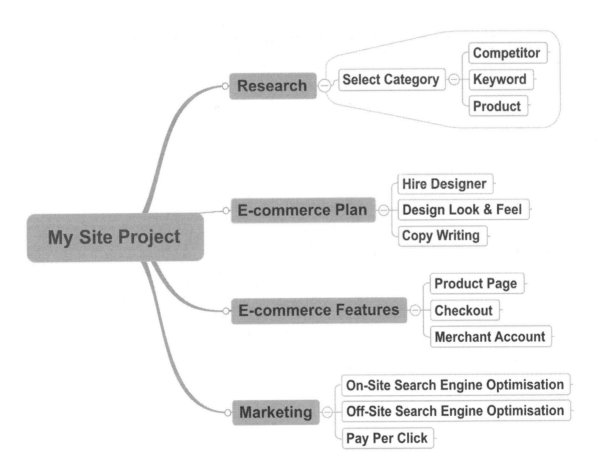

*Example of a Simple MindMap*

## Flexibility.

You and your plan have to be flexible—from the day your website launches—as it is work in progress that acts as a template changing over time. You will not get everything right the first time you implement it and your template will develop as you grow. Decide on a few contingencies for each option and be flexible not rigid, so if you have to move the goal posts you can.

## Time vs. Money.

When you start an e-commerce website and business, there are two possible investment paths or essentially two strategic options to choose from:

- **Option 1 - Time:** Will you start up passively, allocating only a small percentage of the required budget to compete in your product category? Consequently investing lots of time each month for up to 3 years and beyond, before you see a profit?

- **Option 2 - Money:** Will you budget correctly and honestly, and allocate and invest the required amount from day one, giving you the ability to be aggressive and attack your market head on, taking market share from day one?

From my experience and after speaking with clients and other online retailers, I can tell you that the majority of e-commerce businesses choose option 1. I personally believe this is because of: (a) Not planning, forecasting and budgeting; (b) Not being honest with themselves; (c) Fear of failure or success.

You have heard the old adage that essentially says *'You can always make more money, but you only have a limited amount of time'.* This is really what we are discussing here... are you going to join the 97% and invest 3-5 years of struggle, perhaps ultimately quitting with big debts, or do you want immediate profits and success?

## HOT TIP

*Do not be afraid to allocate and invest good money where required, especially in your Start-Up e-commerce website and marketing—It is far easier to start with a BANG and compete aggressively from day one, as opposed to tiptoeing into your market.*

***If You Start Up Passively and Excessively Conservatively, Problems Immediately Become Apparent:***

- Your website is not good enough to compete in your chosen product category
- You have little or no traffic due to poor on-site and off-site SEO and poor marketing

- Your site visitors do not stick... (your visitor-to-sales ratio is shockingly poor) = No Sales!

- Continuous website development and investment is required. Added up over 2 to 3 years this becomes 10 to 100 times more than a solid initial investment would have cost

- As the months and years go by with poor sales, increasing costs and no profits, you get more disillusioned with the time wasted

- You start to panic and invest irrationally in big numbers with little to no return

- *I think you get the idea!*

---

**'To Sum Up This Critical Point...**
*Research – Plan – Forecast – Budget – INVEST – Kick Ass!'*

---

## Budget & Costs.

Decide from the outset what you have to spend, what you can afford to spend and where you should allocate and spend this money. Create a simple spreadsheet using Excel or Google Docs. In the spreadsheet detail what you have to spend as start-up costs, and as you progress over the next 12 months to 3 years. I would focus more on the first 12 months with flexibility. Now detail your business and ongoing costs. Costs are any expense to your business and website, and will include your site build, site maintenance, general business and marketing costs, and outsourcing or employees.

***You Can Split Your Costs Into These Four or More Sub-Categories:***

1) **Product Costs may include:** Buying products, shipping (delivery), and packaging

2) **Website Operational Costs may include:** Initial build & launch of site, ongoing costs for site updates, merchant and transaction fees

3) **Business Costs may include:** Office rental, computers, internet access, insurance and employees

4) **Marketing Costs may include:** SEO, SEM, social media, offline marketing

*Simple Spreadsheet Example:*

| | A | B |
|---|---|---|
| 1 | **Sales** | **Amount** |
| 2 | Product Sales | $300,000.00 |
| 3 | | |
| 4 | **Costs** | **Amount** |
| 5 | Product Purchase Costs | $200,000.00 |
| 6 | Shipping Costs | $20,000.00 |
| 7 | | |
| 8 | Website Costs | $1,000.00 |
| 9 | Marketing Costs | $2,000.00 |
| 10 | Business Costs | $2,000.00 |
| 11 | | |
| 12 | **Costs Total** | $5,000.00 |
| 13 | | |
| 14 | **Gross Profit** | $80,000.00 |
| 15 | | |
| 16 | **Net Profit** | **$75,000.00** |

*Basic Financial Spreadsheet Example*

## HOT TIP

*Include as much as possible of your start-up site development work, features and modules in your initial website build, or you may have unnecessary costs as you grow. Brain dump what you want from the site now, and into the future. Modules and features you do not need when you launch, can simply be deactivated, until you need them on the live site.*

## Forecast for Profit.

When you have detailed your costs and budgets, it is time to forecast your sales. These projections are essentially an estimation based on your research and forecast sales. Be conservative and mark down how many items you predict you will sell per month and per annum, and multiply this by your sell price. Then subtract your Cost of Sale, Materials, Stock Sold, Variable Costs or Direct Costs, and you have your Gross Profit. Then subtract all business overheads (also known as running costs, fixed costs or indirect costs) at the bottom of your spreadsheet and you have your Net (bottom line) Profit. This is the important number that means success or failure!

You now have a good idea if your business and e-commerce site ideas are viable and profitable. Be very honest with yourself as most people fail at this point. Look for any leaks in your numbers and document your actual sales on your spreadsheet, against your forecasted numbers as you start to trade and progress. This will keep you on track.

## HOT TIP

*If you plan on holding stock yourself, as opposed to drop shipping (sending direct to your customer from supplier), these are key costs to include in your forecasts. Holding stock can be very costly when you need to pay for the product up front. Even if you have a monthly credit account with your supplier it will need paying for sooner or later—plus you have warehouse costs and insurance for the stock, etc.*

## Gross Profit %.

I feel it is important to touch on Gross Profit (GP) again as it is something that many online retailers simply have no understanding of.

Gross profit is the profit a business would make after the Cost of Sale, Materials, Stock Sold, Variable Costs or Direct Costs have all been subtracted from your total sales. To simplify: you add up all your sales and then take away all you had to spend in terms of stock or materials, shipping fees to make and deliver those products to your customers.

It is critical to determine if there is money to be made, by working out your GP before you decide on a particular product and market. With online retailing, prices tend to be cheaper than offline. I know that many online retailers try to work with tiny Gross Profit margins. When they deduct all overheads (also known as running costs, fixed costs and indirect costs) from their gross profit, they are left with a miniscule Net Profit or worse still a loss.

Yes, you read that right; many websites are trading at a loss! You'd be better off working for minimum wage than slaving 7 days a week in your own business for a loss.

## Shipping & Delivery Fee Profits.

Shipping charges enable you to make profits on top of your product sale price, so factor this in. If you are charged $5.95 for shipping one item from your courier (Shipping/Logistics Company) you may wish to charge the customer $9.95 as an example. However, do your best to keep shipping fees competitive unless you sell niche and high priced items where you can make really good margins on shipping.

## Seasonal Trends.

When forecasting sales you will need to take into consideration your biggest selling months and your quiet months when sales are low. Depending on the product you are selling, sales will peak and trough throughout the year. No month will be the same and even within each month, you will see a pattern in sales. For example, as and when your prospects get their monthly paycheck, your sales will peak. When you have some trading history and actual data to analyze, this will be essential reading and very important information for you and for your sites' success.

## Handling Growth.

Naturally as you grow your business, sales will rise but so will your costs. This is the challenge, keeping costs low as your sales increase. If you grow fast your costs can so easily skyrocket—and often out of control—on things such as stock, PC's and technology, employees and maybe even a move to larger premises that comes with its own associated costs. So it's critical to keep an eye on your Sales to Costs Ratio. Using good accounts software such as Quickbooks or Sage will allow you to do this, alternatively using a simple spreadsheet will more than suffice.

From the day your website starts trading you must monitor key accounting areas at least weekly - especially your sales and costs, and the resulting net profit (bottom line). Many large companies will monitor these numbers on an hourly basis giving them the opportunity to respond accordingly with product prices, site usability and marketing such is the importance of numbers in your business.

I recommend as a minimum you check your Profit & Loss monthly and your balance sheet weekly.

## Lifetime Value.

In Step 4 of the book, I detail the power of increasing conversions by using Split Testing and Multivariate Testing. The internet allows this testing down to minute detail. Even if at first, results may look too small to *'be worth the hassle'*, bear with me.

The premise of Lifetime Value is that for each new customer you get, their worth in money terms to your company, is calculated over the lifetime of their relationship with you, and not just on the initial purchase. In addition, they may spend increasingly more money on higher priced items as your relationship develops over time.

### *Lifetime Value Example:*

Let's say your e-commerce website sells guitars and you decide to sell a *'Learn Guitar'* book for $10. You pay your web designer to upload a specific page onto your website to promote and sell the *'Learn Guitar'* book costing $100. You then place an advert in *'Guitar Monthly'* which costs you $120. Total spend $220.

From the advert in Guitar Monthly, you then direct prospects (potential customers) to your Learn Guitar book product page on your site. Fifteen people buy the guitar book, which gives a total sales of $150 (15 x $10).

Resulting in Sales ($150) – Costs ($220) = **-$70 Loss**

However this initial $70 loss is acquiring 15 new customers who may go on to buy higher priced items such as a guitar and guitar accessories. The concept is like a *loss leader* in a supermarket where they lose money on the front-end advertised product, to get you to buy more expensive and profit making products when you get deeper into the store.

### Back-End Marketing for Profit:

If you now start to email these 15 customers—as detailed in Step 2 & 4 of the book— and start blogging and releasing product videos, then one or more of these customers will buy again, taking you into profit for this one advertising campaign.

### For Example Let's Say:

  a) 7 of the 15 *'Learn Guitar'* book customers do become long term customers and buy from you each year over a 3 year period

  b) Each customer buys 1 guitar per year during this 3 year period

  c) Guitar cost to you = $150 and you sell for $300 to customer. You profit $150 per guitar sale

  d) 7 repeat customers from the initial advert cost of $70 (which is the total advert/web page cost of $220 less the sale of $150) results in each customer costing $10 to acquire. ($70/7 = $10)

### Evaluation of LTV Using the Above Data:

  – **Formula:** (**a:** 3 years) x (**b:** 1 guitar each per year) x (**c:** $150 profit) – (**d:** $10)

  – **Lifetime Value** per Customer from this one advert campaign = $440

  – **Group Lifetime Value** $440 x 7 = $3080

Your initial disappointment with a loss of $70 now equates to a net Lifetime Value of $3080.

### Lifetime Value Formula Simplified:

  a) Determine the average number of years a customer will buy from you

  b) Calculate the average number of sales a customer will make per year

  c) Work out the average profit you make per sale

  d) Break down the amount of money it costs you on average to acquire a new customer

(a) x (b) x (c) – (d) = Lifetime Value

*We can increase this profit further by implementing the Split Testing & Multivariate Testing detailed in Step 4 of this book.*

## 2) Your Goal & Exit Strategy.

Decide from the start what the goal of your website is. **Ask yourself:**

- Is it to earn you a part time income or a full time income with financial independence potential?

- Do you want to be the leader or authority in your category or marketplace or are you happy to be an average player?

- Will you sell to retail customers only (B2C – Business to Consumer) or will you also sell to business or trade customers (B2B – Business to Business), offering them trade discounts?

- Do you plan to sell to international customers?

- Do you want to become an expert in your products or an expert at e-commerce marketing?

There are no right or wrong answers here, but at least get a concrete idea of where you are heading before you start, and what you will introduce later as your resources grow.

> *'You Will Never Achieve a Successful E-commerce Business—or Any Business for That Matter—Working On Recreational Time!'*

### Time Investment Required.

If you want to maximize your sales, profits and ultimate success, then you need to factor in the time you have available for this project or business from the outset. Do not kid yourself with the time, energy and money that will be required getting to your desired goal. You need to put in the hours, and even if you outsource (delegate tasks to outside companies or individuals) the majority of tasks, you still need to keep in touch and watch your outsourcer team, marketing, sales and profits to remain on target.

### Learning Curve.

Building a profitable e-commerce business requires a learning curve that will take time. Just like learning a new software or skill, the hours just fly by when you are highly focused. So be prepared, accept it, go with it, and do not give yourself too much stick. E-commerce is a big animal, with many processes to learn and refine, so take the positives from the experience and knowledge that you are gaining.

## Product Expert or E-commerce Marketing Expert.

You cannot be both types of expert and effectively maximize profits. Unless you have a massive budget to hire the best of the best in product management and marketing, then being expert in both is unrealistic and not required. I am not for one minute saying you cannot be a leader in your product category or niche.

But decide now, would you rather know everything there is to know about your products—what they do, where they come from, how many widgets they have—or would you just prefer to sell them in huge numbers with as much product knowledge that enables this to happen?

Do you think Amazon are experts with their products, or alternatively are they experts at selling and distribution? Amazon have a data entry system to list products on the website—be it manually or automated—using as much detail, benefits and features as possible, and then use their marketing expertise to sell them like crazy, using Personalization and Recommendation Systems.

So, just to reiterate; absolutely learn your product inside-out where required—if you intend to control your category or niche—so you can write explosive copy that sells, but don't waste the next three years taking a degree course on your products whose only consequence would be to limit your sales. *Marketing aggressively is where profits are at!*

## What Is Your Exit Strategy?

Is your aim to run and operate the website for as long as you can or do you wish to build the website and business up, with the aim of selling in 3, 5 or 7 years? If your exit strategy is to sell in 3 years then detail this in your plan and in your forecasts and watch your targets closely as you progress, to ensure you keep on track and continually increase the value of your website.

## Website Valuation.

At the time of writing, websites sell for around 1–2 times Net Profit Earnings so bear this in mind. Net earnings are what the site makes in Net Profit in twelve months. Many publications will tell you that you can get anywhere from 3–12 times net earnings but in my experience aim for 1–2 times net. Maybe you can get more for the next YouTube but not for a profitable *small-to-medium* size e-commerce website.

## Selling to International Customers.

Selling globally can add a huge increase to your sales volume and net profits with a potential audience of billions. Run the research for international customers using the research tools detailed in *'3) Do the Research'*. When you look at your site user stats, you will be surprised how many international prospects actually visit your website.

**Note:** You need to watch the exchange rate closely when selling overseas and determine if you can buy products competitively enough to compete with suppliers in the country of your shoppers. VAT may also apply.

## Trade Accounts (B2B).

Offering trade customers—business-to-business (B2B)—the option to buy at discounted prices can further boost site sales. You can give discounts by a set amount or set percentage. By way of a simple trade application form on your website, you can entice trade customers to apply for a trade discount and get them into the e-commerce trade module in your Content Management System (CMS) back-end. You manage your trade specifics and applications in there.

You can then approve the account and set the required discount for each specific trade customer. Communication with your trade buyers is also possible, with regards their approved discounts to their specific accounts, via automated emails, synchronized with the trade account. Additionally you can set credit card only accounts or even offer 30-day credit accounts, whereby 30-day invoices are raised and emailed automatically.

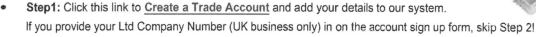

How to set up your Trade Discount Account in 2 Easy Steps:

- **Step1:** Click this link to **Create a Trade Account** and add your details to our system.

  If you provide your Ltd Company Number (UK business only) in on the account sign up form, skip Step 2!

- **Step 2:** Once your account is set up, send us your Business Letterhead to verify your trade status. We will then switch your account to Trade!

  **UK customers** fax your letterhead to: ▮▮▮▮▮▮

  **International customers** fax your letterhead to: ▮▮▮▮▮▮

  **OR Email your letterhead here**

- Once your account is set to Trade you can take advantage of very competitive single and multi-buy prices. **However there is no minimum order quantity.**

*Example of a Trade Page With Account Application Link On a Live Website*

*Example of a Trade Application Form*

# 3) Do the Research.

Before you start an e-commerce website, it is critical you put in a good day's work and do the research. **Competitor, Keyword and Product Research** all need to be carried out to prevent you entering a market where there is little or no demand (prospects) with potentially too much supply (competitors)—or just the fact that the product you intend to sell has a market, but that market is not online. Having discipline and putting in the research time now can prevent years of headaches, pain, and stress and ultimately save you a lot of cash in the process.

What if you **do** enter a market with a small amount of customers and lots of competitors? This may equal disaster—unless you totally dominate this niche. However, *'niche'* too often equals to *'small a market and small profits'.* You want to enter a niche category within a big product category. Such as *DVD players* as a niche category within the main *Home Entertainment* category.

## Competitor Analysis & Research.

Competitor Analysis is about assessing the strengths and weaknesses of your current and potential competitors—finding your competitive edge—and has two primary objectives:

1) Obtaining information about important competitors

2) Using that information to predict competitor behavior

36

### The Goal of Competitor Analysis Is to Understand:

- Which competitors to compete against and to go head-to-head with
- Competitors' strategies and planned actions
- How competitors might react to your market entry and subsequent actions
- How to influence competitor behavior to your own advantage

Simplified, this means you need to go to the Google search engine and start looking at your future competitor's websites.

### Ask Yourself These Questions:

- Are your competitors' websites good or poor quality?
- What products, features and services do they offer?
- Who comes up in the top 10 search results for your top keyword terms?
- Is their On-Site (On-Page) and Off-Site (Off-Page) SEO work of high quality or mediocre?
- Do they advertise with Google Adwords (Pay per Click) or focus on search engines only?
- How many ads do they run and do they have a large budget?
- Can you compete, give them a good run for their money, and take sales and market share from them?
- What is your Competitive Edge, your Unique Selling Proposition (USP), where can you excel where your competitors do not?

There are various tools available to carry out solid competitor research prior to launching your website, and also once you are trading. These allow you to watch your competitors' behavior, including their site and product updates.

### Tools to Help You Monitor Competitor & Market Activity:

- Google Alerts: www.google.com/alerts
- Copernic Tracker: www.copernic.com/en/products/tracker/index.html

## Keyword Research.

Use the keyword tools on offer—such as Google's free Google Adwords Research Tool—or use a subscription service like Wordtracker.com as these will give you a good idea about the market you are about to enter. This involves running searches for your top keywords, seeing what online searchers are actually typing into the search engines, analyzing the results and making your product decisions or site content based on this.

When you have the data, mix these numbers with your common sense and intuition. And I say this because you may find some keywords that you absolutely know are major search terms, are showing as low volume on the keyword tools.

My best advice here is to go to the two sites below, read the help files and simply have a go, and utilize the export to CSV (or Excel) option. You will soon understand what they are about and this will give you a good overview of your market supply and demand.

- Google Adwords Tool: **US:** https://adwords.google.com/select/KeywordToolExternal **UK:** https://adwords.google.co.uk/select/KeywordToolExternal
- Wordtracker: www.wordtracker.com

## HOT TIP

*When exporting to CSV or Excel, before you sort the key phrases into your desired order, insert a new column in A and number the key phrases top to bottom. This helps you to reorder the spreadsheet and key phrases into the original exported order, should you wish later on.*

### Product Research.

Just like with competitor research, get out onto Google and see what products your competitors are selling and the price they sell them for. You will soon get a good picture of what sells and what does not and if there is profit to be made. Tie this in with your Keyword research and you will establish what products your prospects are searching for (demand). Worldwide brands are just one popular product research tool found online:

- WorldWideBrands: www.worldwidebrands.com

# 4) Where Will You Provide Value?

Business is a value for value exchange. Therefore, the question is; can you do things exceptionally well and give your customers great value and the WOW factor? Many e-commerce websites and businesses are mediocre at best, in all areas from design to customer service. What is your competitive edge? Where will you excel and go that bit further than your competitors?

## Price Is Not Everything.

Do you have a Unique Selling Proposition (USP) and offer something your competitors do not? If it's a lower price, remember that being cheaper does not always mean you will get the sale. Every potential customer is different and people have different buying personalities that can fluctuate. Many people do not want cheap and cheerful products, so a lower price is only good for some people and some products but not for others.

Perception and perceived value also comes into this equation. Find your target customer and sell to them at the recommended price. Ask your supplier for their thoughts on price. By testing various prices—on the live website—will show you within a week, what your best sell price is, by the number of sales made.

# 5) Who Is Doing What In the Business?

Do you intend to handle everything yourself or will you have employees and will you outsource some of the tasks? Will you be holding and handling stock (inventory) or will you use a fulfillment center (also known as a fulfillment house), that can do just about everything for you, from taking phone calls, handling emails to delivering products to customers and even handling returns?

An e-commerce business needs you to Source, Stock, Sell, Ship and Support your products. You may need outside help.

## Outsourcing.

Outsourcing simply means giving a specific role or project to an outside company or individual. Many of the outsource websites including Elance.com, Freelancer.com or ODesk.com have a plethora of people waiting to handle your project.

However a big word of warning; the majority of providers are *'yes men'* and will claim they can do anything you ask or give them. But in my experience of using over a 100 different outsource companies or individual's for various projects from logo design, through data entry to web development, I can guarantee you that at least 70–80% are mediocre at best.

Am I saying all outsourcers are bad? No, and you could effectively run your whole business this way like the very successful Double Your Dating company does. What I am saying is this: take your time hiring someone and select outsourcers with a high positive feedback and absolutely interview them (or grill them even) prior to hiring them. Do not pay any money up front until you have worked with them and are happy with their skills (where possible), and get them to sign a contract that covers various points. See *'Hiring a Web Designer'* in Step 3 for more on this type of contract.

## Time.

Typical daily e-commerce projects or tasks include: web design and development, sales, operations, customer and technical support, copy writing and web content, images, data entry, marketing and SEO.

So take into consideration what you or your team can handle and how you can save time, energy and money by outsourcing, employing staff or by using a fulfillment company. Outsource and fulfillment companies will even handle operations such as order processing, product shipping, returns and refunds. However, I like to keep a few of these operational tasks in-house to ensure the service provided is optimum.

Many outsourcers are self-employed *'individuals'* that are also employed fulltime elsewhere, so bear this in mind when hiring them. If you have timelines to meet with regards completing areas of your project or launching the website, etc., then all targets need to be agreed and documented—in the contract prior to starting.

# 6) Sales & Customer Support.

Exceptional Sales and Customer Support—also known as Customer Service—is the foundation to every successful e-commerce business. A Sales Person is the frontline contact with prospects before they buy—and contact to your company is by email or phone. Customer Support is after the sale, again by email and phone—if you offer this option. I recommend you offer phone sales & support as it says so much more about your company than those who hide behind email. If required you can use separate phone numbers for sales and support.

> *'The Way You Handle Customer Sales & Support Enquiries Can Seriously Affect Your Reputation and Consequently Your Sales.'*

## Response Time.

Statistics suggest that on average a customer will visit up to seven websites prior to making a buying decision. Of those seven sites, they will email approximately 30 percent with a product enquiry and questions. The interesting thing is they copy and paste the same email question to each website awaiting a fast response. Customers have no loyalty to one website.

So, aim for the WOW factor! When a prospect emails your sales department, the faster you reply, the better the chance of converting this enquiry into a sale ahead of your competitors. Respond in minutes where possible and aim for under an hour.

## Attention to Detail.

If you take your time to read customers' email enquiries and respond to all questions and points raised, with speed and accuracy of responses and with politeness, then in my experience they will buy from you and forget the rest. When I have personally emailed companies for information I estimate about 50%–70% actually read and responded to the email exactly, some gave blunt answers and many did not even answer some of the questions. This just causes frustration for the prospect and the sale is lost.

Being an online marketer I have spent a few bucks to bolster my own education with the big US based Internet Marketers - these guys utilize clinical sales funnels to sell products. However, when you contact their customer support desks or email support—from my experience and from all accounts reading the forums online from many other people's experiences, (just search for *'[internet marketer's name] scam'*)—the level of support these guys offer is pretty poor to say the least.

Contrast this with a reputable e-commerce company such as Amazon.com. The support you receive there is exceptional—in my personal experience.

So would I recommend a company that offers poor customer service? Absolutely not! Would I recommend a company where I had a great buying & support experience such as Amazon? You bet I would!

Therefore, this *'word of mouth'* advertising, positive or negative is critical to your bottom line profits. I am sure you have heard the saying *'When you have a good experience you tell your close friends and when you have a bad experience you tell everyone'*. This is Word of Mouth Advertising in action.

## Word of Mouth (WOM).

WOM Marketing can promote and even explode your business, spreading like a virus, and simply because you *'did the right thing'*.

You've heard of viral marketing, like when a YouTube video spreads like a virus—and has millions of views in days just because it's *'funny'* or *'weird'*. The same thing can happen on a smaller scale, if you can convert an unhappy customer into one who is delighted with the way you responded to their support query and resolved their problem fast. They will rapidly swing from a negative emotion towards your company, to one of highly excited sales person! You have to see this in action to believe how powerful it can be. So where possible, help and resolve customer queries fast, sticking to your principles!

Networking is a driver of WOM and should be implemented continuously as you grow.

## Customer Problems.

In Step 1, *'Thirteen Common E-commerce Mistakes'* I touched on not being a slave to your customers' demands. To elaborate on this I want to mention customer mindset. Everybody on this planet has their own problems—including your customers—and their current mindset and personality is determined by current events. For example if your customer has booked a day off work to receive their order—and the courier fails to deliver for whatever reason— this can be the final straw, the trigger for your customer to lose it! They then phone you up and give you or your team an earful of their frustration.

However, customers can also get worked up over very minor things. So as soon as you can, decide on a rule or measure to what degree you will stand for any bad attitude, bad language, insults and unacceptable behaviour to protect your employees. I do not say this to scare you, but it can happen occasionally. If you've done everything right— apologized, explained the reasons why and taken the appropriate action to resolve the problem and fast—and the customer still insists on being awkward or using abusive language, then maybe you need to terminate the relationship!

## Rule of 3.

In my office, my team and I decided to practice a Rule of 3. This essentially gives the customer three chances. We at first apologized and explained how we would resolve the issues promptly. Then if the customer continued to raise their voice, swear and be verbally abusive, then we would repeat our recommended course of action, looking for the customers' cooperation. On the 3rd insult we would simply say *'OK, here's what I would like you to do, please package the product up securely and return to the address I'm about to email you, Thank you, Goodbye'* and end the call.

You may think this is not required for your business and this is fine. However, what you will quickly learn is that when a customer is in a negative state of mind, the law of attraction swings into action and everything continues to go wrong for them. As an example: if they have received a faulty product and you then send a replacement—you will find the replacement will not get there in one piece. It is as if they make it happen!

You will not get many of these customers but when you do, they can drain staff morale and sap your energy and enthusiasm so fast. Ultimately, your job is to provide exceptional quality products and service. Your job description does not include insults or verbal abuse from customer—regardless of your customers' *'problems'.*

## Support Center Software.

When you launch your site, you may want to start with a simple contact form and traditional email. However, once you get more traffic—and as a consequence more sales and support enquiries—using good support software and modifying it to fit your business can give you big advantages over your competitors.

## Customer Community Support.

A trend that is growing fast online is customer community which is a way of sharing information with others, giving full transparency. Many businesses including Amazon, Dell, Google and Kiddicare.com now use a mix of marketing, customer support, social media, R&D to build a transparent and open-book customer community.

This allows companies and customers to work together. Through this you can create a real-time social knowledgebase that connects customers with each other, your company, and the answers they're seeking.

## Support Center Customer Benefits.

Good support software keeps things organized. Emails - also known as Tickets - are all located in one area with a secure login. You will maximize efficiency, email enquiries can be answered faster, and all history per contact is logged. Customers can select the website and/or department they require from drop downs menus on a webpage, if you have multiple websites and departments.

## Support Center Company Benefits & Features.

Good software like this also has secure individual user login so all email/tickets are assigned to each specific user. You get all kinds of statistics and features; all of the support emails are split by department and/or website, the senders' full details, time, comments, which employee responded, your notes, plus more. It's all tracked. All of these processes can be automated, synchronized and even outsourced easily.

In addition, if you have multiple websites in a network as I did, this enables all websites to link to the one support center for easy management. You can also display best selling products on the support center home page, so when prospects or customers contact you for *'Pre-Sale'* enquiries they may see an attractive deal and place an order. When the contact form is submitted, the prospect is presented with a contact *'confirmation page'* just like you get after placing an order and having gone through the checkout. This is where you can position newsletter email opt-in forms, RSS subscriptions, special deals, best sellers, and links to other sites, and so on.

## Outsource Sales & Support.

Additional benefits are; you can outsource the support to an outsource company or individual that is accessible via the web 24/7. I had two fulltime employees in India running my sales and support center, handling the support and technical support enquiries for one of my site networks. This worked very well and they synchronized perfectly with my employees in the UK sales office.

## *Popular Support Center & Customer Community Software:*

- Kayako: www.kayako.com (paid)
- eTicket: www.eticketsupport.com (Free - Open source)
- GetSatisfaction: www.GetSatisfaction.com (paid)

I have used all of the above software products and all can be modified to fit your specific needs, some more than others. Kayako has more features, but is more complex to use and modify. I spent a bit of time reworking eTicket support to fit my exact specification and prefer to use this now as it is clean, simple and does all I need with the option of flexibility if I need to make changes. GetSatisfaction is ideal for a website selling products which create lots of social conversion such as health products.

**Parking Dynamics Sales and Support Contact Form**

**Sales, Product Advice, Support and Technical:** The Parking Dynamics PD1 product has detailed and in depth info on the website. If you stil have further questions please complete the form below to contact one of our advisers who will endeavour to respond within the hour. Please allow 1 business day if contacting us at the weekend. *To View Your Open Support Enquries scroll below the Contact Form.

**Contact Form**

| | |
|---|---|
| Select Department: | Sales Enquiries ▼ |
| Your Name: | * |
| Email Address: | * |
| Confirm Email Address: | * |
| Phone: | |
| Message Subject: | * |
| Message Details: | |

d867k

Security Code: _____ * Enter security code above in box. This is to prevent spam.

Submit

**View Your Open Support Enquiries**

| | |
|---|---|
| Your Email Address: | * |
| Your Enquiry Ticket ID: | * |

Submit

*Support Center Contact Form Page With Option to Check Open Ticket Below*

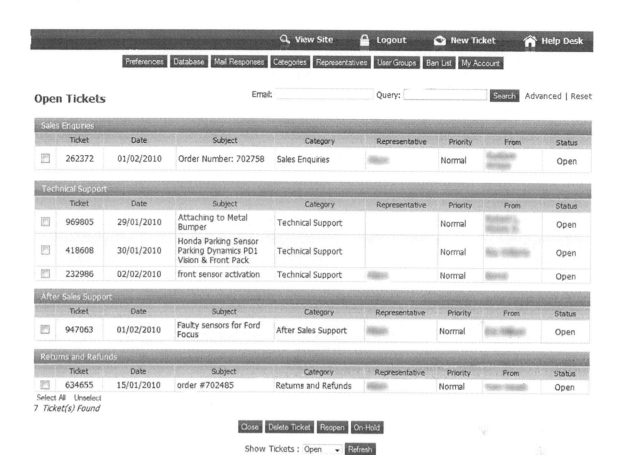

*Support Center Main Admin Screen Using eTicket Software*

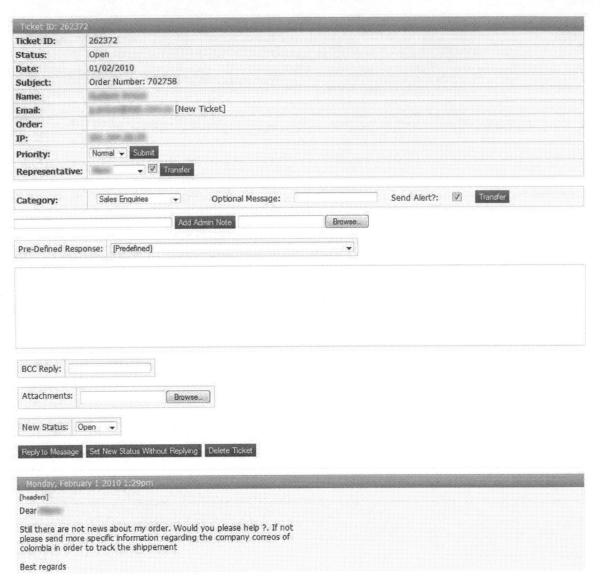

*Support Center Individual Ticket Screen In eTicket Software Admin*

### Popular Live Chat Software:

I won't say much about these as I recommend you check out the different live support companies in Google; features and prices change often between the different software brands. My favorite two out of the ones I have tried are:

- Live Person: http://solutions.liveperson.com/live-chat
- PHP Live: www.phplivesupport.com

My preference is Live Person although it is quite expensive for a start-up website. I would only recommend you use this software product when you get more visitors.

Live chat software can build trust quickly as customers know they can reach you rapidly and immediately. Live Person offers some great statistics like those offered by Google Analytics. I also like to use Live Person because the chat window is 100% secure, so you can take orders from customers through this window.

*Note: I recommend you negotiate on price when you speak with your Live Person representative; they always bend on price to get your order.*

## Email Reliability.

Monitor your email delivery rates with feedback from customers. Get a feel for your email reliability on a regular basis, run tests, and check to see if customers are receiving it. Is your email being blocked by their email client spam filters or worse is it being blocked on their servers? I have had experiences where the email service provided by certain hosting companies has been blacklisted by customers because of spam issues in the past. If your emails are not reaching customers' email inboxes, then communication and sales will be negatively affected.

# 7) Product Buying & Management.

To source product suppliers and distributors you can start offline by looking in retail and trade magazines, visiting trade shows, and approaching local and national brick and mortar companies. Online you can start with companies such as WorldWideBrands.com, or just search on Google for your products, using terms like *'MP3 Player Distributor'* or *'MP3 player trade suppliers'*.

*Popular Product Source Tool With Integrated Research Tools.*

- WorldWideBrands: www.worldwidebrands.com

## Considerations When Selecting a Product.

*If You Have Not Yet Decided On a Product Range to Sell, Consider the Following:*

- Is there profit in the product?

- Will your supplier grant you (full) exclusivity on the product?

- Is the product patent protected?

- Customer demand: what is Your product life cycle until people stop wanting it?

- Supplier: are they reliable, how good is their warranty & returns process, what are their long term plans?

- Is support and technical help available from your suppliers and how (email, phone, live chat)?

- How big is the product range? are new products planned?

## Buying Products.

When buying products, always start by asking your suppliers for trade price lists and bulk buy tier structures as they often give bigger discounts if you buy in larger quantities. When you are ready to order, always negotiate on their prices and ask what *'special deal'* you can have for buying in bulk quantities. Tell them you intend to shift a boatload so you get a great deal. As your business grows and you spend more with your suppliers, continue to negotiate on price at least every 3-6 months.

## Gray Imports or Replicas.

The internet is a hot spot for gray imports and replica products. A gray import is the genuine product, but sourced from a foreign market where prices are typically a lot cheaper and specifications are sometimes slightly different. The biggest issue with *'true'* gray imports (not knock off clones or replicas) is the manufacturer's warranty and whether this is honored. Gray market items are predominantly sold on the internet or through wholesale channels where it is difficult for the buyer to properly inspect the product prior to buying.

## Product Warranty.

Establish the warranty period of each product. For example, many products come with a standard 12 months manufactures warranty. Generally, gray imported products will not have warranty cover. Therefore, it is important to clearly establish the warranty and returns process as inevitably some products will break down.

### Check the Following With Your Supplier:

- Does your customer return directly to wholesaler or manufacturer?
- Do they return to you and then you return to wholesaler or manufacturer, or is there a third party company that handles or repairs your product?
- What are the timelines, logistics and costs on the above scenarios?

## Number of Products.

Decide if you will sell a few products, hundreds of products or even thousands or tens of thousands of products. Selling fewer products results in less work and gives you more of a niche positioning of your e-commerce website. However, on the flip side the more product pages you have in Google or the other search engines, the more entry points your prospects will have, and the easier it will be for them to find your site.

## Product Data Entry.

You can do this yourself or you can outsource this laborious process. If you outsource you may need to modify and improve the descriptions later—to add a sales edge. You will need brochures, images, descriptions and prices (where available). Your supplier may have all these in a spreadsheet CSV file, so you can import them directly into your e-commerce back-end admin for maximum speed.

## Data Feeds.

Data entry of your products and real time stock updates of your products can be automated, if your supplier or distributer offers this service. Data feeds are a way of integrating a real time stock database—commonly including products descriptions, images and prices—from your suppliers' main system into your website.

This is an ideal tool if you do not hold your own stock, and makes for optimum efficiency. Whenever your suppliers update the stock or prices change, this is change is immediately reflected in your website's stock level numbers, and in real time on your live website. The large computer component companies use this model to keep on top of the rapid changes to stock levels. To do this manually—if you don't hold your own stock—would be next to impossible, or would require full time employees in house or outsource, working around the clock.

# 8) Drop Ship, Hold Stock or Fulfillment.

Before you set up your e-commerce website you will need to decide if you'll be holding stock, drop shipping your products (delivery direct from your supplier to customer) or using a fulfillment service for handling any aspect of the operations process (pre-sales to shipping).

## Hold Stock.

If you hold your own stock, you will need money to invest in this up-front, unless your supplier offers a monthly credit account. In addition, you will need a warehouse or stock area and all the necessary insurance. Depending on your website model—if you have live online stock levels—you would also add to this a stocking system linked to and displaying real time stock levels on your live site, and a shipping and tracking system all synchronized by your e-commerce back-end admin.

## Drop Shipping.

This simply means sending products direct from your supplier to your customer. When you get an order, you will email, fax, set-up an RSS feed or order online - on a secure trade area - or phone the order through with customer details to your supplier who then drop ships the product direct to customer. Where possible get a daily report of items shipped from your drop shipper so you can then inform your customer that their order has been shipped and also to keep your records updated.

If you drop ship you will not be offered quantity-buy discounts on products. However, buying drop shipped products at a discount is definitely achievable if you *negotiate*.

### *Drop Ship Discounts Are Achievable:*

1) If you buy and ship in single orders, the total will accumulate over time, equivalent

to a one off bulk buy

2) If you buy in bulk and store these products at the drop shippers' premises

You can choose to hold stock (shipping products yourself) and drop ship products where required. This depends on the products, supplier, shipping costs and the money available to purchase stock.

**Problem:** Your supplier may accidentally or intentionally put his company name on the shipping label that your close trade competitors may get hold of.

**Problem:** Your supplier mistakenly includes your trade invoice in the box—that your customer then receives. This does not look professional and a tough one to explain.

**Solution:** Stipulate in advance to your drop shipper that you **categorically** *'do not want any company labels on the packaging'* and *'No Paperwork in the Box'* when they ship your products.

## Ordering Products.

You can place product orders from suppliers via email, fax, online, via an RSS (XML) feed or by phone: in bulk, or in single units from your drop shipper. This can be done in real-time (per order) or at the end of the day. Using Excel or an RSS feed is a great method for simple automation. Data you will send will include your customer's name and shipping address, along with the item and quantity required. For maximum efficiency and productivity, you can set your e-commerce system to synchronize your orders with your suppliers using one of the above methods.

Your customer will still receive the order invoice via email automatically from you when they order, so you essentially have a paperless office and everything is seamless.

### HOT TIP

*Some suppliers may charge a fee 'per item' for providing a drop shipping service. Also be aware if you choose to buy in bulk and store at the drop shippers, they may want to charge you for this. If they do negotiate, remember that you are selling their products and that they should accommodate your set-up and processes where possible!*

## Fulfillment.

Some companies—known as a fulfillment center or fulfillment house—normally independent of your suppliers, will do and handle everything for you: from taking phone calls, answering emails, holding and delivering stock to handling returns. Some fulfillment companies also manufacturer specific products such as books, CDs and DVDs including the branding and artwork for the packaging.

These services come at a price and may reduce your profit margins too far to justify using them. Check with your individual product suppliers to see if they can integrate and offer you these services. Even if they do not offer it currently, they may make an exception for you, especially if you sell in large numbers. My suppliers did!

# 9) Shipping & Logistics.

I recommend that you decide what shipping options, methods and services you plan on offering to your online customers, before you start on your website development.

- Will you use one shipping company or multiple ones, depending on the products you are selling and the country you trade in?
- Will you use the national postal service as a cheaper option?
- Alternatively, will you give multiple service, price and country options?

Speak with a few shipping companies, get price tariffs, and ask about bulk shipping discounts, and what targets you can aim for as you grow and ship in higher quantities. The more you ship, the cheaper each delivery will cost. Also, establish who your competitors use, and other sites you like and trust for ideas.

## Shipping Costs.

You need to weigh up the shipping costs you charge to your customers. Decide if they will be free and absorbed in the product price or if you will charge an extra shipping fee on top of the product price. What shipping services will you offer? *'Next Day Guaranteed'* or a slower service, and will you give various price options? Offering different shipping options gives customers flexibility, as many people are at work Monday to Friday, and may only want their product delivered when they take a specific day off. A next day shipping option would give them this flexibility.

## HOT TIP

*You may make savings on shipping fees if you ship the products yourself, this can make a huge difference to your profits.*

## Failed Delivery.

Things do not always go to plan when using third party shipping companies. So expect it, and be ready to get reimbursements when things go wrong: weather delays in winter, busy periods like Christmas and holidays, broken down vans, loss, theft, etc. All of these and more can affect shipping times.

If your customer is out when your courier attempts delivery, you will normally get 2 to 3 more attempts at no extra charge, before your product is *'Returned to Sender'.* You can then resend the item to your customer—but be sure to bill them again for shipping, as your courier will charge you. Detail this in your website shipping terms and conditions in the help or support section of your site.

## Shipping Options.

The more shipping options you offer, the more complex your website shipping module will be. So plan ahead, get all the required data into a spreadsheet and hand this to your site developer to import into your site, and things will run smoothly from here. In the shipping module, you can stipulate different prices, different services (Next Day, 2 Day, 1st Class, and 2nd Class), different countries and different weights.

### *Popular Courier, Shipping & Logistics Companies:*

- DHL: www.dhl.com
- Fedex: www.fedex.com
- Interparcel: www.interparcel.com (The world's top couriers in one place at the most competitive prices)
- Post Office.com: www.postoffice.com (Postal Services in each country)
- Royal Mail: www.royalmail.com (UK Postal Service)
- UPS: www.ups.com
- USPS: www.usps.com (US Postal Service)

# 10) Returns.

It is important to check for any distance selling regulations and returns policies for your specific country, and to detail them on your website. In the UK there is a 7-Day Distance Selling Regulation called the *'Consumer Protection (Distance Selling) Regulations 2000'.* This means a customer can return a product within 7 days, if bought online or by mail order. This is called a cooling-off period and must be detailed on your website—usually in the help or customer support section. Many online retailers or customers are not aware of such return policies.

## Money Back Guarantees.

In addition to this standard 7–day policy, I always give at least a 30–day or more Money Back Guarantee for one simple reason; it removes the perceived risk from your customer's purchase and builds trust, resulting in more sales. You may not have to give as much as 30 Days or more. Try 7 days, 14 days, 21 days, 30 days or more and test the returns and refunds percentage. However, highlight the guarantee that you give on your website to build immediate trust.

In many tests offering and advertising an explicit *'No Risk Money Back Guarantee'* suggests the risk is removed from your customers' buying decision, and more sales are made as a result. Refund rates will be different for each product, customer type, market, business positioning, website, sales and quality of after sales support you provide.

## Reduce Returns.

Offer and honor your returns guarantee. However, you do not have to make it too easy to return goods; how you do this is entirely up to you. For example, I would advise against displaying your returns address on your website. This would make returning goods too easy, and your systems would not be able to track returns efficiently.

Moreover, this is not for anything other than to ensure that a customer wishes to return the product for the correct reasons. I say this as many customers struggle with the most simplest of products or procedures; be it set up problems, operation or technical issues, looks too complex, didn't work, I can't install it, installation costs too much, etc. So help them out with their product issues and your returns rate will plummet.

## Returns Process.

My websites have a returns process in place giving the customer every reason to keep their product. I say this because they really want to keep the product. The process goes like this. A customer raises a returns request—through the *'returns'* link inside of their user account. They are then presented with a confirmation page. On this webpage it explains; why they shouldn't return the product just yet, what the top five technical issues are and how these can easily be resolved, where to find PDF manuals to download and where to find help guides and help videos in the support center pages. In addition, an email is automatically sent to them, with the same information.

You can track your returns in the back-end site admin area, or by spreadsheet, and a returns rate percentage should be determined, on a monthly basis at least. My average returns rate across multiple websites was 2.7%, and the internet average for physical products I believe is 5–10% plus. When you establish your returns rate, you can then hone and refine your returns process to get it reduced by any means possible.

### HOT TIP

*A good idea is to sell Returned products for less than normal price on your website in an 'outlet' or 'closeout' section and/or on eBay. If you haven't already set up an eBay account or for a small monthly fee an eBay business account with a store. I like to sell all returned products on eBay at cost (trade) price. This keeps products moving and prevents money being tied up holding inventory (stock).*

## Suspected Faulty Products.

There are various ways you can handle this. You firstly need to establish if the products you have sent are indeed faulty. The majority will not be. So using the ideas above ensure your customer goes through your problem resolution process, has access to help guides, installation guides, Troubleshooting and Fault Diagnosis guides and videos where possible. In addition phone them up if required.

My employees or I often phoned customers up directly to establish *the reason for return* and to help sort the problem out fast. Do not be afraid to speak with customers. Often a quick call can sort a problem in minutes—this will result in them cancelling their return request and profits from the sale remain in your bank account.

## Replacement Product for Testing.

Depending on what products you sell, sometimes you will need to send out a replacement product or perhaps just an individual part only. In such a scenario, you can do one of two things.

***Option 1: Send the replacement product or part in good faith at no cost to the customer.***

- Here you need to stipulate what to do if the product is in fact faulty and how and where to return it—to you or to your supplier

- Stipulate a return by date for either the faulty product or the replacement

- You need to detail that if the faulty or replacement is not returned within X days (mine was 30 days) you will bill their card accordingly

- They must return the faulty or replacement product to you using a tracking number for their protection to insure against loss or damage. You could even send them a pre-addressed padded envelope bag. I did in some cases. But if it has a big box, don't bother

***Option 2: Send the replacement product or part and bill the customer.***

- Stipulate that upon receipt of the faulty or replacement product you will refund them in full

- Stipulate a return by date for either the faulty product or the replacement

- They must return the faulty or replacement product to you using a tracking number for their protection to insure against loss or damage. As in Option 1, you could even send them a pre-addressed padded envelope bag. depending on the type of product and its original packaging

## Collecting Products.

If you wish, you can offer free returns like many catalogue and clothing websites offer. Just make sure to factor this into your prices and evaluate how much it costs you in returns employees and software to handle this—as you will definitely get more returns as a result. You could even offer a collection service for customers, be it free, or at a cost to the customer. This will definitely give you a Unique Selling Proposition (USP) but will also cost you time, money and employees to operate smoothly!

## Repeat Return Offenders.

The need to reduce returns is important to reach higher profits. Typically, 80% of your returns will come from 20% of your products. So establish if specific products are breaking down and if they are, consider dropping them from your range if they are serial return offenders. Then investigate further to see if you are getting returns because customer support is poor, for example. Are your emails excessively slow in response? Do you ignore the phone for long periods of the day, with the result that your customer's trust has waned? Do you need to include more install and technical manuals or PDF's in the box or on website as support? All are important areas to look at.

## RAM Number.

A Returns Authorization Number (RAM Number) is generated by your e-commerce software returns module, and is your way of tracking customers' returned products. If your product range does not a have high returns rate, this system may be unnecessary. Many return requests can be reversed by phoning customers to assist them—as mentioned above—in addition to advertising on your website that a RAM number is a mandatory requirement before they can send the item back to you. This is because to get this number they must follow a *'step-by-step'* returns protocol exactly. This gives you the chance to assess, address and reverse their request for a return.

### HOT TIP

*If drop shipping, establish what your suppliers' returns policy is for faulty products. If customers send items to you, make sure you have enough space available to store them.*

# Legal Considerations for Selling Online

The law in your specific country and internationally is an essential consideration when planning to sell products online. Each country has its own legal rules and terms. The list below uses the UK as an example, *but I recommend taking professional advice from the e-retail industry bodies in your country.*

### *A Brief Overview of Items That Are Often Within Distance Selling Regulations:*

- You must give clear and detailed information about the goods and services you offer on your website, including product prices and shipping

- When a customer has ordered you must send them conformation. This can be in way of an automated email acknowledgement

- Delivery of products should be made within 30 days of the order date, unless otherwise stated

- Your customer has the right to cancel an order within 7 working days (Monday–Friday). This period runs from the day after the delivery date

- The effective date of a cancellation is the date on which your customer raised the cancellation with you

- Your customer must cancel in writing, be it email, returns process on your site, by letter or fax

- A refund must be actioned as soon as you can but within 30 days maximum

- You can request that the goods are returned within a set period or as soon as possible

- You can collect the goods yourself via courier if agreed, be it at a cost or free of charge

# Multi-Channel Considerations

Are you planning to sell both online and offline? This is multi-channel trading.

At the time of writing E-commerce accounts for over 30% of all retail sales worldwide and demonstrates that mixing the two sales channels can be explosive when working in synergy; especially when you run marketing strategies such as '*Buy Online, Collect-in-Store*'.

***When Trading Through Multi Channels There Are a Number of Elements to Consider When Building Your Website and In Preparation for Hiring a Web Designer and Employees:***

- What overall budget are you allocating to the initial setup of your website? Have you compared this with existing and similar live websites, ensuring it is a realistic figure?

- Are you planning to offer the same, selected or additional products on your e-commerce site compared to your offline store?

- Will you be synchronizing your online and offline prices to between website and offline systems at all times, including sale periods?

- How much overlap will there be between your online and offline sales operations, deliveries to stores and returns to stores?

- Will you be offering a Buy Online, Collect-in-Store service?

- What shipping options and methods do you plan to offer your online buyers and will these be additional to your existing arrangements?

- Have you budgeted for all online and offline running costs and how will you measure the profitability of the site against that of your offline channel?

- What contact points will you have on the site? For example, an address and landline phone number is important for credibility

- How much time have you budgeted for testing the site before going live?

- Will you be selling to US, UK, Europe or Worldwide and do you need to consider setting up international languages and currencies?

- Do you have a compelling launch event planned to promote the tie-in of your new site with your existing offline business, which will attract the local press?

- An e-commerce website should be updated often. How will you manage and coordinate design and product updates between your online and offline operations?

# Planning Your Website Development

Before you start building your e-commerce website, let's take a closer look at the essential elements and software options at your disposal. These are choices that will mean long-term success or imminent failure.

## Web Design & Development: In-House, Outsource or DIY?

There are four main e-commerce software and technology options available to you when starting an e-commerce website project. With some good, robust and reliable pre-built systems available, you do not have to reinvent the wheel.

## Four E-commerce Software Solution Options:

1) **Boxed-Solution.** When you purchase '*out-of-the-box*' software, you create your own pages possibly from basic templates in the software, add the content and away you go. Sounds easy and it is, but your site will stink! Not recommended if you want big sales and big profits. You will need to invest many hours amending your website, constantly trying to improve the design, usability and operation. The reality is that there are very real limitations to how your site will look and perform. So select this option only, if you are on a very tight budget, and enjoy hard, laborious work.

2) **Custom (Bespoke) Solution.** Build a Custom and Bespoke e-commerce website to fit your exact needs, by using an external design company. This method starts by giving a specification brief to establish your requirements and because the company is starting from scratch, your site can cost up to five times that of using a branded solution as in number three.

3) **Branded Software.** Use established and reputable e-commerce branded software, built and designed by an external e-commerce specialist company. This is my recommended option for a website that delivers on all your feature requirements, for the best investment. However, not all e-commerce software is created equal, so you need to follow the information below.

4) **In-House Team.** Use an in-house team or employees and resources available to your company. Generally, this involves building a bespoke site from the ground up. This is often perceived as the more cost-effective solution if your company already has an IT team with web design and development experience. However, you will quickly find out the costs frequently outweigh the profits using this model. Employees, plus hardware, plus software can easily exceed $160K (£100K) in year one.

### Software Options 2 and 3.

Using an external web development company to build your ecommerce website, requires you to decide upon and hand over a specification list of the features and modules you require to your short listed companies, allowing them to give you a *'Yes or No'* on your requested feature list. *Each company will then respond with a quotation based on your site spec.*

# Software Recommendation?

I have used three boxed-solution e-commerce software, three branded software, and one bespoke e-commerce system. The branded software option is my personal preference when you make it exactly as you want it, by adding your own bespoke elements—if these are not already included as standard. I have experienced exceptional results customizing and super-charging the popular osCommerce software with bespoke modules and features to fit my specific website needs.

## Etaila.com

Is an e-commerce solution being developed by the team that built my power-house osCommerce sites mentioned above. It is based on the **Traffic > Conversion > Relationship** model and will integrate a feature-rich spec needed to dominate any market. Features include Search Engine Optimization, Conversion, Multiple Checkouts, Split Testing, Key Reports, Product Page Features with Multiple Templates.

However there are many other great e-commerce branded solutions on the market now including the popular Magento.com and you will quickly learn what to look out for in the following pages. All you have to do is (1) decide on your budget, (2) highlight the features you want, (3) hire a designer and get your website started.

*Your Required E-commerce Specification and Web Designer Skills Can Include Any, Perhaps All, of the Items Below Taken from an Exhaustive List of Features and Modules Available:*

**Forecast Traffic & Sales.**
- – Projected Monthly Traffic
- – Projected Turnover

**Site Layout & Structure.**
- – 3 Tiers: (1) Home Page > (2) Category Page (thumbnail view/page) > (3) Product Page
- – 4 Tiers: (1) Home Page > (2) Category Page > (3) Sub Category Page (thumbnail view/page) > (4) Product Page

**Site Design.**
- – Colors, Alignment, Text, Font, Images, Layout, Usability
- – Logo: New or Existing

**Product Information.**

- How will You Provide the Data (Spreadsheet, CSV, Direct Data Feed)
- Number of Products You Intend to Sell
- Details of Options and Variants (Color, Size, Length, Weight, Wattage)
- Images (Detail, Quality, Number, Multiple Images Per Product)
- Videos Required
- Product Resources (Print Page, Email Page, Bookmark Page, Share Page, Rate Page, Shipping Details, Customer Reviews, Product Comparison Feature, Product Warranties)
- Wish List, Customer Notes

**Shipping Options.**

- Shipping Companies, Method, Number of Services
- Countries
- Costs

**Stock.**

- Data Feed
- Real Time Updates
- Linked with Back-End Systems

**International.**

- US, UK or Multiple Currency Option
- Multiple Language Options

**Operations.**

- Order Processing
- Email Management
- Customer Support
- Returns Management
- Sales Linking to Accounting Software
- Contact Form, Support Center, Live chat
- Email Newsletter

**Marketing & Social Features.**

- RSS
- Blog

- Social Modules, Sharing Tools

- Discount Code Vouchers

- Personalization - Recommendation Engine & Systems

- Multiple Front Ends with one Back-End for Multiple Sites with Maximum Efficiency & Productivity

**SEO Features.**

- Meta: Page Titles (Title Tag), Description, Keyword, H1, H2

- No Follow Attribute Option

- Automated SEO Processes (Linked from Product to SEO Modules)

**Community Tools.**

- Support Centre, Customer Q&A, Customer Reviews

- Blog, Forum

**Reports.**

- Products Viewed

- Products Bought

- Best Selling Products

- Google Analytics

# Flexible Branded E-commerce Software.

Selecting Option (3), a flexible and branded solution, gives you many benefits. They include the option of taking a demo test drive before you invest, and seeing a live e-commerce site that already uses this tried and tested software in action. Add to this that you will be delegating all technical work and processes to specialists that use this software day in, day out and you're onto a winner from the start.

*Consider These Aspects (Why Option 3 Is My Favored Software Choice):*

**– Look and Feel.**

- Choose exactly how you want to position your website, category, brand and products

**– Navigation, Layout and Structure.**

- Allows you to build the site perfectly for your users, and for the Google search engine

**– Search Engine Friendly.**

– Build your site and structure to work in harmony with Google and not against it

**– Stock Availability.**

– Flexible options to handle products, stock, and accounting

**– Products, Pricing, Images, Descriptions, Video.**

– Keeps and automates your site data current, and displays with full product functionality

**– Sales Funnel, Shopping Cart and Check Out.**

– Takes a customer by the hand from site entry to exit in as few steps as possible increasing sales

**– Order and Customer Management.**

– Delivering products on time, every time with optimal customer communication

**– Analysis, Statistics and Performance Reporting.**

– Specific, detailed and up-to-the-minute user behavior data and reports

**– Visibility and Backup.**

– Guaranteeing your e-commerce website is online 24/7, with reliable hosting and daily backups

# Resources Required.

The following tasks will need to be assigned to one or more of your project managers that are handling your project. Assign the tasks according to the person best able to get the job done, while also making the best use of that person's time.

- Site Design and Development
- Content Creation
- Data Entry
- Stock Management
- Customer & Order Management
- Operations & Email Communication
- Shipping, Drop Shipping & Fulfillment
- Security and Anti-Fraud Measures
- Analytics, Reporting & Statistics
- Data Security & Backups

- Returns and Faulty Goods
- Online Marketing
- Offline Marketing

### *Example Mind Map of a Website Development:*

As previously detailed, using planning software such as Microsoft Visio, MindManager or even Microsoft Excel allows you to have a visual and structured plan to follow. This will keep your web designer on track and ensure delivery time lines are met. However, keep it flexible as things do not always go to plan.

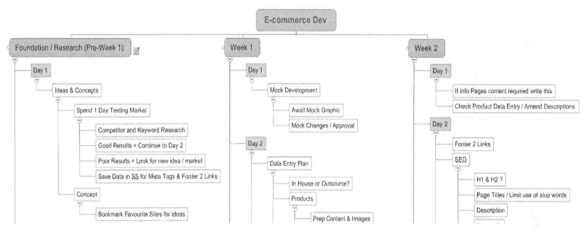

*Example Project Outline & Timeline Using a Simple MindMap*

***In Step 2 We'll Discuss the Key Elements and Resources Needed for Building and Producing a High Performance E-commerce Website That Sells Products In High Numbers. The Last Thing You Want Is a Pretty Website with a Lousy Conversion Rate!***

# Step 2—
# Get Sales

## Build & Launch Your E-commerce Website - Fast!

→ Discover the Key Elements of Highly Profitable E-commerce Website!

→ How to Design Your Website for Rapid Sales & Profits!

→ Increase Conversion Rates By Up to 300%!

→ How to Set-Up & Integrate a Merchant Account!

→ Why You Must Know Your Customer Better!

→ How a Revolutionary Checkout Removes Resistance & Increases Sales!

→ Use On-Site (On-Page) SEO Factors for a Google Assault!

→ How to Maximize Your Order Confirmation Page!

→ Site Launch Essentials!

→ 5 Pre-Launch Testing Requisites!

# Key Elements of an E-commerce Website

To build and launch a successful e-commerce website there are many elements and skills required. Every area must be as strong as the next, or the weak link will let the whole business down. Think about this; you have a store in a virtual location that must attract and convert visitors into buyers. You must approach this differently than you would a regular offline store.

A successful project requires the input of website designers, developers, graphic designers, conversion and usability specialists, and on and offline marketing and retail professionals. They will all contribute to your website. Once you have learned and internalized the *'insider'* information within this chapter, you have the tools to launch a highly profitable e-commerce website.

## 1) Domain and Hosting.

A successful e-commerce website starts with a good domain name also known as a URL (Uniform Resource Locator), and good branding based on your product, category and positioning. I recommend that the first step you take when selecting your domain name is to include your main keyword or key phrase and then brand it. Unless you have a few hundred thousand dollars to brand your website each month, then do your best to build a brand from day one, by adding a great, memorable and recognizable logo to your domain name. This does not have to be costly, but remember that a good domain name, nice logo and great sales and support will stand you in good stead.

*3 Quick Examples from Websites I Built and Used to Own:*

1) CarAudioPlus.co.uk - where *'Car Audio'* = key phrase, and *'Plus'* = brand

2) iPodCarKitDirect.co.uk - *'iPod Car Kit'* = key phrase, and *'Direct'* = branding

3) InCariPod.com - a perfect domain name as it is a top key phrase in itself and also great for branding

---

*'A Few Online Marketing 'Gurus' Will Tell You That It's Not Important to Have Your Key Phrase In Your Domain Name, But In My Intensive Testing, This Advice Is Wrong'*

---

*Why You Need to Use Your Main Keyword In Your Domain Name:*

1) Your website will be easy for customers and prospects to remember, if your main industry product phrase is within your name, especially if it is short and succinct

2) The second critical reason for having your top keyword, or key phrase in your domain name is all about incoming links, especially free or (natural links). Links (real name hyperlinks) are the Holy Grail when it comes to SEO, and getting above your competitors in the search engines. Links are detailed later on in the book, but essentially the more links pointing to your website, the better

People may link to your website—because they deem it a good resource for their website visitors—from blog, forum and social site chatter. If you follow this tip and place your key phrase in your domain name then you will automatically get good high quality links. This is because people linking to your website will frequently use your website name in the link text itself. This text in the link—what people click on to get back to your website—is called the *'anchor text'.*

Search engines often attach more importance to a link if the anchor text is directly related to the theme of your site via a relevant keyword, which is the case when your domain name, containing the keyword, is included in this anchor text.

## Selecting a Domain Name.

It's tough when selecting a domain name, especially if you want a .com, .co.uk or other top level domain (TLD), for your particular country, as many have already been registered.

When creating a name do your best to keep it as short as possible - 3 or 4 words maximum—and make it memorable. Use your keywords and branding as detailed above, and if you are using more than one word—and where feasible—look at using a theme like *Best Buy, Coca-Cola or Weight Watchers.* This is called *'Alliteration'* and these names are highly recognizable and memorable!

For example you could be *'OnlyOrganic.com', 'FitnessFirst.com'* or *'CoolCarComponents. com'.*

## Buying Domains.

I can make two recommendations on where to buy your domain names: US based, or internationally, buy them from GoDaddy.com. Based in the UK, buy them from 123-reg. co.uk. When you have registered your domain name, you can then forward the *'Name Servers'* to where your website is hosted making your website live. This ensures you remain in full control of your domain name now and into the future. It is essential you retain full ownership of your domain name at all times.

- GoDaddy: www.godaddy.com (US and Global customers)
- 123 Reg: www.123-reg.co.uk (UK customers)

## Hosting.

Select a reputable host for your website to ensure you get good bandwidth, good load speed, maximum uptime and visibility. You need your website to stay live and online 24/7/365. The company that designs your website may even provide hosting, which many companies do. However, ensure their support response is rapid if your site ever goes down, or if you need help with something else site-related.

Research and read customer reviews online for good *'uptime ratings'* to get some feedback, prior to signing up to any specific company.

# 2) Design.

When selecting a designer or design team—see Step (3) for hiring tips—it is important to be aware that not all web designers are equal. Choose the right designer and watch your profits soar. Choose the wrong designer and experience 6–18 months or more of sheer frustration, just waiting for your new website to be built and launched.

Your website design is the main element in determining if visitors will stay or leave. On entering your website you will have 5–7 seconds to hold your visitors' attention or they will *'bounce'* and will be gone forever *'CLICK'.* So help your visitor make the *'should I stay or leave'* subconscious decision into a positive *'I want to stay'* emotional experience by following these guidelines below.

## Alignment.

Absolutely use Cascading Style Sheets (CSS) for the navigation and site templates. This means that any changes such as color or menus can be implemented and updated across the whole site in seconds, without the need to update every page individually.

Use clean lines and boxes with straight or round edges, and group items such as text or images in small boxes or small blocks on the web page for easy scanning. Use small text headlines for each block—if appropriate—so the eye can easily scan your site pages without getting confused with one big splash of information, with too many links and options.

When a visitor is reading or viewing your website they are using *'Foveal Vision',* which is the sharp central vision—the small area you focus on at any one time. So grouping items as above is perfect for quick scanning of your pages and data assimilation.

## Colors.

Use a design and color scheme appropriate to your brand and positioning. If you sell eco-friendly products then you will look at using green colors and if you sell bathroom products, use blues. As a foundation to these colors use a white background—lots of white space—so your text is clear and your images are easy to see and have visual impact. Think Google's design philosophy and simplicity. This contributed to its rapid success as a search engine.

A clean, almost neutral design, with one or two accent colors works very well for most e-commerce websites. Look at Amazon.com and Cruthfield.com for good examples. And remember: people are there to buy your products, not admire your fancy graphics, so let your products do the work.

### *Use Your Color Choices Wisely:*

- **Blue** - Blue is often associated with depth and stability. It automatically evokes emotions of trust, security, intelligence, peace, and loyalty in people. Blue is the color of the ocean and the sky and is proven to work well when promoting air and sky products (airlines, air conditioning units, fans, air filters) and water and sea products (cruise vacations, water filters, boats, bottled water, bathroom products)

  *On the other hand, avoid blue when promoting food and cooking products.* Blue suppresses the appetite

- **Black** - Power, class, seriousness, drama, sophistication, and boldness (works well for prestigious products, stylish homeware, photography)

- **White** - Purity, peace, cleanliness, freshness (works well for medical products and weight loss products)

- **Purple** - Sophistication, royalty, mystery, spirituality (works well for yoga products)

- **Green** - Freshness, safety, growth, vitality, calmness, prestige (works well for drugs, health and wellbeing, medical products, natural products and eco-friendly products - use darker green for financial or make money products)

- **Orange** - is used to evoke enthusiasm, fascination, happiness, creativity, determination, attraction, success (works well for toys and puzzles)

- **Red** - is often associated with passion, desire, war, danger, strength, power, and love (red works well in the dating and seduction niches, and it also works well with products such as energy drinks, automobiles, and items related to sports and action)

- **Yellow** - is an attention getter, which is the reason taxis are painted this color. When over-used, yellow can have a disturbing effect. Tests show that babies cry more in yellow rooms. *Yellow* is seen before other colors when placed against black, which is why this combination is often used to issue warnings or for strong branding

  Men tend to see yellow as a lighthearted, *'childish'* color, so it is not recommended to use yellow when selling prestigious, expensive products to men. This explains why you very rarely see Yellow in high-end watch advertisements, or advertisements for expensive cars

## Buttons & Internal Links.

Websites and the web itself is just one big network of links. All pages on a website are connected by button, graphic or text links. So think carefully about the shape, color and wording on your button links, as different emotional responses are evoked. Test this using Google Analytics and Split Testing—detailed in Element 15 and Step 4—to see if visitors actually click them or ignore them. If you use graphic links, accompany these with a text link where possible. For optimum SEO use keywords or key phrases—again where possible—in the internal link (anchor text) on your website.

## Graphics & Images.

For that initial *'hook',* use stunning and professional images and graphics where possible. Your website graphics will blend nicely with your website design and text. Do not use too many graphics and again let your product descriptions do the selling once the visuals have evoked an emotional response.

Speak with your product suppliers to get good product images, as they may have already had these created by professionals for brochures, and other marketing. Images can graphically paint the emotional result that your product gives to your prospect, and really entice them to feel the experience they will get by owning your product.

Also use Alt Text on your images, so if the image does not load—or is slow to load—your visitor knows what is supposed to be there in the blank space. You can set-up your e-commerce system to automatically extract the alt text information, from your product Name Field and display this with each image—for ultimate automation.

*Image Type.*

- **Homepage Images:** Do not use too many images here, just enough to get your prospect hooked and into your deeper category and product pages. If you have a lot of content—for SEO purposes—then more images may be required to balance out the copy

- **Thumbnails:** These are the smaller preview type images and are good to use on the product category pages, detailing the products in this particular category—or naturally the *'thumbnail'* page, if you are using a thumbnail page. Also used on the product page as related images, so when you click or hover on these, they appear bigger in place of the main image or in a new window

- **Main Product Image:** Use the highest quality image you can find (while still displaying correctly in customers' browsers), as this is crucial for evoking positive *'I want this product now'* emotions and experiences in your prospects mind that initiates an immediate buying response

- **View Larger Image:** Great so your prospect can see your product in closer detail. Typically opens in a new or pop up window. It's essential to have a clearly worded *'Close'* or *'Close Box'* link in this window, so your visitor can click it and close the window, and get back to buying your product

- **Magnify (Zoom) Image:** Allows your site visitor to zoom in on any area of the product—ideal for clothing. Only use a good and fully tested magnify/zoom module—as many you see on websites are often flakey—and only add more resistance when they fail to work properly

## Logo & Branding.

Use a professional and easy to read logo, with pertinent colors and font styles for your business positioning. Look at the elite and successful companies in the world and you will see how clean and simple their logos are; such as Amazon, Dell or Walmart. Place your logo, top left of your website in the header, and think about a short tagline underneath using keyword rich text so Google can read and index it for SEO purposes.

Link your logo to your full URL (domain) http://www.yoursite.com when clicked. Also set your logo to display *'homepage'* when a visitor hovers their mouse over it, but only when you are on any page other than the homepage. See Amazon.com for ideas.

## Load Speed & Headlines.

If your web developer can do this, load the center of your website first where your headline and intro text sits. This center area is the *'Center Container'*, and it loads faster than the main site template (Header, Footer, and Side Columns). By loading your center container and text headline first, it will capture your visitor's attention, especially if it's benefit-oriented as in the following example:

*'iPods, MP3 Players & MP3 Accessories All At Exclusive Prices*
*and Delivered to Your Door FREE, In 1-3 Working Days'.*

This makes your website *'sticky'* and encourages visitors to want to stay on your website especially if your images are slow to load, or if your visitor's internet connection is slow. Images and graphics–such as your header and footer–can sometimes take up to 30 seconds to load, and if they are set to load first, but don't, then your customer has no benefit to hold them and may leave.

People are trained to read bigger, bolder words... so make your headlines bigger and bolder. Make them red, if and where feasible, so they stand out from the rest of your text. However black and dark grays are more professional for ecommerce stores.

Give your sub-headlines and paragraph titles a bit more emphasis than your regular body copy. And use plenty of white space, so your page doesn't look crowded. For headlines and sub-headlines, try fonts like Impact, Tahoma Bold, and Helvetica Bold.

*'Keep It Simple, and Create a Consistent and Familiar Hierarchy With Your Content; Headlines, Sub Headlines & Descriptions On All Pages.'*

## Description Text & Fonts.

Write descriptions that are interesting, informative and loaded with benefits. There is a debate with e-commerce websites where *'gurus'* say it's wrong to use long descriptions. In my experience, this belief is wrong. If your products and customers require a lot of detail, then use long copy split into sub-headlines and tables. This is great for SEO!

Use clear text on navigation buttons and on product menu lists with a capital letter at the start of the word, and lowercase thereafter (Start Case). I would definitely not use all CAPS in product menus too often, as CAPS ARE HARDER TO READ than a Capital Letter Plus Lowercase (Start Case). Nor would I recommend using just lowercase throughout the buttons and links—unless that is your theme and it fits.

## Easy to Scan.

Layout your text descriptions so your pages can be scanned quickly, from top to bottom. The use of a main headline, sub headlines and splitting areas of your content into headers or tables with headers such as Description, Features, Specifications and Technical Data going down the page, allows for quick scanning.

## Accessibility.

Use a clean font style appropriate to your website, product, category and themethat is easy to read and use the appropriate font size for your user. If you are selling to an older age group, think about using a larger font or even explicitly give the option to view with larger font—as not many people know how to increase the font size in their browser. Many websites set up a unique page called Accessability for the visually impaired with options to increase font size and in some cases change color backgrounds and fonts to suit.

*Basic Button Examples of How to Offer Different Font Sizes On Your Website*

## Fonts.

Try Sans-Serif fonts for your headlines and sub-headlines, and Serif fonts for your regular in-line body copy. Sans Serif fonts are clean and straight fonts *without* those little extras on the tops and bottoms of the letters. Serif fonts have the extra little embellishments.

For your regular in-line body copy, use Serif fonts. Serif fonts have been used in print for years (Magazines, Newspapers, Books) and have been proven to create higher readability. This includes fonts like Courier New, Georgia, and Times New Roman.

## F-Pattern.

Eye tracking research suggests people read websites differently than books and magazines—that is, top to bottom and left to right. Instead they read a web page in an F-Shaped pattern which is in horizontal '*sections*', and read less and less of each line as they read down the left side. So position your important site elements, such as product menus and site navigations at the top and on the left hand side.

## Marketing & Promotional Elements.

Use these areas and boxes to promote your special offers, best sellers, email news letter opt-in, security info, technical info, trade info. You can position them on the main navigation bars as regular links, in the center container on the homepage or footer as on-page graphical elements, or as commonly seen in the left and right hand columns below the product menus.

Keep this information small in height, position it in square or round edge boxes, and use clean colors that are subtle and not too overpowering. Let your main site navigation and features control the website sales funnel, and allow your marketing areas and boxes to balance with the site design and be available if your site user needs them.

## Main Website Table Position In Browser.

Do you position your website in the center of the page (on the screen)? To the left of the page? or do you consume the whole browser window like Amazon.com does as an example? This really is personal preference and there is no right or wrong table positioning.

### Consider These Points for Your Site Table Positioning:

1) Consider the screen resolution size used by your customers, so it balances well on screen

2) The amount of products your website sells and the number of services you are promoting. If these two are massive like an Amazon.com, then utilizing the full screen is recommended, so you have enough room to promote everything. On the flip side, if it's cluttered then it can be very detrimental to usability and conversions

3) Length of menus and marketing & promotional boxes that you need to display in the left and right side columns such as opt-in box, security and cards, ordering, best sellers, trade service, or whatever it may be for your particular site and the services offered

4) Your target visitor and size of font and content required. People with impaired vision may need the font larger with less clutter

5) Carrying on from (4), do you need to focus the website on a narrower width to give the eye a cleaner and simpler area to view?

6) People read from left to right, so for a more traditional audience, a left aligned table layout may be more appropriate

## Attention to Detail.

Be detailed and specific, clean up typos and grammar. One spelling mistake can give the impression that you do not check things. If you cannot spell, or cannot be bothered to check your spelling, a customer will doubt that you can handle their credit card and personal details responsibly. These are subconscious thoughts and references that customers make.

# 3) Usability.

A clean, clear and simple navigation layout, with multiple navigation and product search options is the way to optimize usability—and consequently maximize sales.

## Know Your Customer.

If you do not know who your customer is, find out - and quick! We'll discuss this in more detail shortly, but in order to maximize sales and conversions you need build your website specifically for your target customer.

## Demographics & Psychographics.

This is simply about communicating to your audience effectively. Every personality type, every age group (within reason), every intelligence level and every internet experience level can land on your website. Have you considered building your website for the visually impaired, so they can easily navigate? How about providing how-to guides and help videos, to educate your users? These are just two simple examples to get you thinking.

## Multiple Languages.

Offering multiple languages and selling globally can on average add 25% to your sales. This obviously depends on the product you are selling, and its suitability to be shipped overseas. However, having a global reach gives you and your customers a win-win situation.

Ask your web developer if they have a stable and reliable multi-Language module, and can you see it in action on a live site. Many branded e-commerce software solutions now come with this option. When testing on a live website, look for any text overflow in box headers and descriptions, as words can be longer when converted into other languages.

## Google's Free Website Translate Tool.

Google offer a Website Translator module that can be integrated into your site in minutes, by way of a simple piece of code. This will add a simple drop-down menu to your site, in your chosen location, and will provide your site users with approximately 50 different language conversions.

**Note:** Any text overflow present, when your default language is converted, is something you may just have to accept. So weigh up any negative effect of this text overflow versus the simplicity of using this module, and the extra sales you could get as a result of selling globally.

- Google Translate Tool: http://translate.google.com/translate_tools

*How Google Translate Tool Will Look On Your Website*

## Trade Accounts.

By way of a simple trade application form on your website—similar to a contact form but with company details—you can offer trade customers a discount on products. Trade customers complete the form and their details are then stored in the e-commerce trade module, in your Content Management System (CMS) back-end, awaiting your approval. It's all managed there.

## Contact Forms.

As discussed in Step 1 (Sales & Support), using a clean and simple contact form is essential, so that would-be-customers can reach you easily. I prefer contact forms to displaying an actual email address on the live site, because spammers can get hold of your email address. If you add a CAPTCHA challenge response (security code) onto your contact form, any spam attempts are blocked.

**Contact**

Complete your details below to contact us and we'll endeavour to respond within the hour.

Your name: *

Your e-mail address: *

Phone: *

Subject: *

Message: *

CAPTCHA
This question is for testing whether you are a human visitor and to prevent automated spam submissions.

S N e l

What code is in the image?: *

Copy the characters from the image.

Submit

*Example of a CAPTCHA Enabled Contact Form*

77

## Search Box.

All good e-commerce websites must have a search box option, as this is one of the first features a user will look for when entering your site and searching for products. More often than not, prospects will have arrived at your site direct from the Google search engine where they will have used the search box feature. So give them consistency and offer a search box.

**Note:** Test your search feature for accuracy of search results, before making your website live. If you give poor search results to your visitors—as many low-end e-commerce solutions do—you will deny your prospects and customers access to your product offerings and frustrate your site users.

> • See Google's Commerce Search for ideas: www.google.com/commercesearch

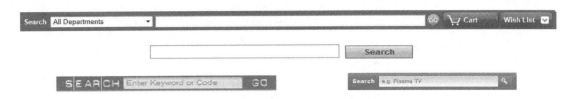

*4 Search Box Examples*

## Easy Navigation & Product Menus.

Finding products easily is down to using a clear hierarchy of product tiers, using text links or buttons to navigate from the home page down to the product pages. This clear structure is critical so your site user knows where to click to find the products they want. Use clean and uncluttered product menus and navigation bars. If you have a long product menu, split this into groups with a small heading per group so that it's not one long—hard to read—menu.

***Give Various Navigation Options So Customers Can Easily Find Your Products:***

- Use a simple search box that scans your products for matching keywords

- The header navigation bar can have a *'Shop'* link/button linking to a page with all your product categories listed all on the one page

- Alternatively use a header navigation bar with a drop down menu displaying each main category or subcategory

- A left hand product menu can detail each product category or subcategory, using text or graphic headers for each and as in the paragraph above following a linear path to the products

- Taking navigation to its optimum level, a filter module giving the savvier net user a way to drill down through product attributes, to find specific products in seconds

- Thumbnail page (category or subcategory) will have sort features to filter by type, price, date, amount, alphabetical order, or even most popular, and the ability to ascend & descend these options and a '*View Items Per Page*'

- Product promotions on your home page or left or right hand columns – for example Top 10 Best Sellers, New Arrivals, Sale Items.

- You can position Best Sellers and New Arrivals in your main site header navigation bar for optimal prominence

- Footer Links provide quick access to specific categories or direct to specific best selling products (this is a good strategy for SEO too)

- Link to your products from your Blog, How-to Guides, Videos, Product Reviews.

In the example below, you will see that the silver menu in the center is made up of collapsible lists. When you click one of the main bold categories a list drops down to reveal the products within.

*4 Easy to Read and User Friendly Product Menus*

## Highlight Categories.

When a site user is in a specific category on the website, highlight this on the navigation bar so they know exactly where they are on the website at any moment. This can be by way of a different shade of button or an underlined or bold font. Alternatively, use detailed header text to show in what category they are currently located.

## Breadcrumbs or Breadcrumb Trail.

The small horizontal links positioned at the top of product pages—directly below the header navigation bar—give users a way of keeping track of the path they have taken, and show them their current location within your e-commerce site. *The term comes from the trail of breadcrumbs left by Hansel and Gretel in the fairy tale; as they go deep into the forest, they drop breadcrumbs to help them find their way out.*

Breadcrumbs are very useful on deeper e-commerce websites that have lots of categories, products and pages. It is your decision if you want to use them. Some websites do, some do not. *They can be used for navigational purposes, and also as an advanced SEO strategy.*

Most sites use these poorly. This means that a large percentage of e-commerce shoppers do not know what they are, or what they do. If you are using these for user navigation then do exactly that, showing people their current location on your website. It is important to highlight that the breadcrumbs are navigational links and can be clicked—instead of having these small but very useful links camouflaged.

I'd even recommend highlighting the breadcrumb link of the area of the site they are currently in, like this below highlighting the Product:

**You Are Here:** Home > Category > **Product**

The breadcrumbs in the images below are all located at the top of the website product and category pages, directly below the main site header. The iHerb.com example (bottom of the 3 breadcrumb images below) highlights your location in green.

home > mens > tees & polos > digit tee

▸ **You Are Here** > In Car iPod > Dension

Brands A-Z > Now Foods
Brands A-Z > Now Foods > Now Foods, Vitamins > Now Foods, Vitamins A & D
Categories > Vitamins > Vitamin D3

*3 Example Product Breadcrumb Trails*

# Checkout Breadcrumbs:

Using a breadcrumb trail in your checkout process is highly recommended even if you opt not to use one for your product hierarchy. This is detailed more in section 5 entitled '*Checkout*', further down the book.

The top two breadcrumb images below are positioned at the top of the checkout page. The bottom 2 images are both used on the same checkout pages. The text in bold, '*You are Here*', sits at the top of the checkout pages and under the site main header; the small round icons sit at the bottom of the checkout pages. *You can be flexible and also use one or the other, either at the top or the bottom of the page.*

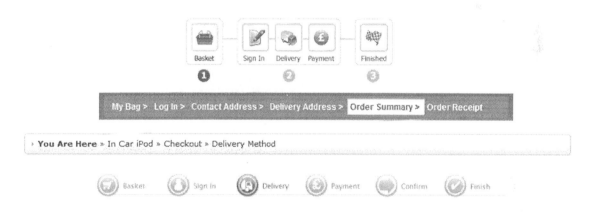

*4 Checkout Breadcrumb Trail Examples*

# Sales Funnel – Guide Your Visitors.

If you want people to buy your products, take them by the hand from entry (entering your site), to exit (ordering a product): either explicitly tell them exactly what to do within each step, or make it so obvious and self-explanatory that nobody could miss it. This is your sales funnel. Good e-commerce websites have them. If a customer lands on your home page, then subtly guide them to your category page as fast as possible, then into your product page, and then into your checkout with as few steps and as little resistance as possible.

# Website Product Hierarchy.

E-commerce websites follow a hierarchy or tier structure, like a tree with branches. However, if you go deeper than three clicks—from the home page— before you get to a product page, you will lose visitors and Google will struggle to find your products for ranking and SEO purposes. To get it right, there are typically two popular product hierarchies used on e-commerce websites.

*Recommended E-commerce Website Tier Hierarchies:*

1) **3 Tiers:** 1. Home Page > 2. Category Page (or thumbnail view page) > 3. Product Page

2) **4 Tiers:** 1. Home Page > 2. Category Page > 3. Subcategory Page (or thumbnail view page) > 4. Product Page

## 3 Tier Product Hierarchy.

If you have a DVD website for example, you would structure it like this.

**Tier 1 - Home Page:** The Home Page is the top tier and displays your products by category on the product menu links. When a customer clicks a product menu category (such as Comedy, Drama, Sport), they enter into the Category Page (also known as a thumbnail page)

**Tier 2 - Category Page:** All products within this specific category will normally be laid out on the page using a thumbnail view. This is like a preview of all of the products in this one category page using a small thumbnail image per product, maybe a small intro description, possibly price and customer review rating and a *'view more'* or *'learn more'* (or similar) button. When you click the thumbnail products link or image, you enter into the main product page for that particular product

**Tier 3 – Product Page:** This is the product page where the customers will *'add product to cart'* before entering the checkout. You will display main product images, description, features, price, Add to Cart (Add to Basket) button. on this page. *See Element 7 for Product Page information*

## 4 Tier Hierarchy.

If you have a clothing website, you could structure it like this.

**Tier 1 - Home Page:** The Home Page is the top tier and displays the products by main category on the product menu links. When a customer clicks a product menu category (such Men, Women, Children), they enter into the Category Page

**Tier 2 - Category Page:** Here the categories will display sub categories from within the main categories such as (Men's: T-shirts, Shirts, Knitwear, etc.). When a prospect then clicks a product link such as T-shirts, they enter the Subcategory page (also known as thumbnail page)

**Tier 3 – Subcategory Page:** All products within this specific category will normally be laid out on the page using a thumbnail view. This is like a preview of all of the products in this one category using small thumbnail images, maybe a small intro description, possibly price and customer review rating and a *'view more'* or *'learn more'* (or similar) button. When you click the thumbnail products link or image, you enter into the main product page

**Tier 4 – Product Page:** This is the product page where the customers will *'add product to cart'* before entering the checkout. You will display main product images, description, features, price, Add to Cart (Add to Basket) button. *See Element 7 in the following pages for Product Page information*

***On the Next Page See Example of a 3-Tier E-commerce Product Hierarchy...***

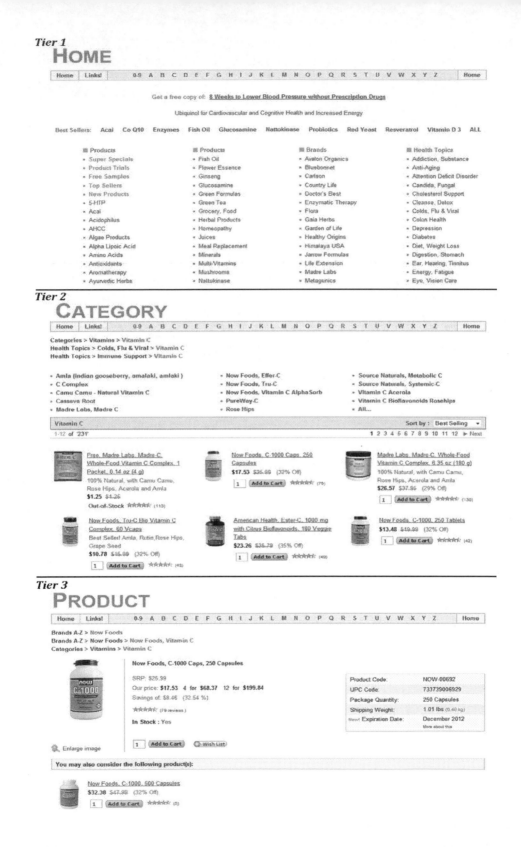

*3 Tier Hierarchy (Home, Category & Product Pages) from iHerb.com*

## Sort Feature.

It is critical within the sales funnel process to offer usability options to your prospects and existing customers, but you must make it seamless. Category (Thumbnail pages) must provide various sort-filtering options that could include:

- Sort by Type
- Sort by Price
- Sort by Color, Brand or other specific
- Sort by Date Newest added to Site
- Sort by Best Selling
- Sort by Amount in Alphabetical Order
- Ability to '*Ascend & Descend*' all of these options
- View Quantity of Items Per Page'
- Most Popular or Best Selling

**Sort By:** Type, Price, Date, Amount, Alphabetical Order—This enables customers to quickly find the product they want—then you can get them into the product page so they can place an order.

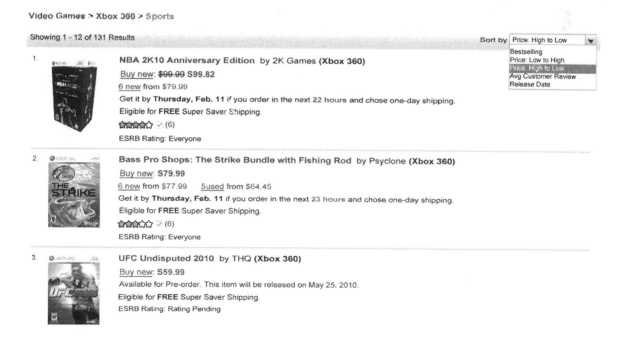

*'Thumbnail View' Category Page With Sort Feature Showing Various Options*

**Parrot Bluetooth & Handsfree Car Kits**

Bluetooth Car Kit Direct only Retail Official Parrot Merchandise which is covered by the Parrot Guarantee. See below the list of parrot products in stock & available to purchase. The Parrot Minikits are universal bluetooth car kits while the CK & MKI range are hard wired options providing excellent quality and feature rich functionality

Displaying 1 to 8 (of 8 products)

| More Info | Brand/Model/Type | R... | Price | Basket |
|---|---|---|---|---|
| | **Parrot Minikit**<br>Parrot Sun Visor handsfree Kit - Universal Bluetooth | £6~~9~~ | £49.97 | ADD |
| | **Parrot Minikit Slim**<br>Universal Sun Visor Bluetooth Handsfree Kit from Parrot | £89.99 | £69.97 | ADD |

Sort By: Price: Low to High — Items Per Page: 20 (10, 20, 50, 100, All) — Pages: 1

*Thumbnail View Category Page With Sort By, View Items Per Page & SEO Content Above Using H1 Tag On Blue Title & Keyword Rich Description*

## Two Popular Shopping Cart Processes.

When customers *'Add to Cart',* there are two common methods used by e-commerce websites. It is important to test each before selecting a model to follow. We'll discuss more on this testing (Split Testing) in Step 4.

**Standard Cart Process:** When a customer adds a product that they want to buy to their cart, they are automatically taken to the Shopping Cart page (as the image below shows). From here they can click *'Continue Shopping'* that will take them either back to the product page they have come from or to the home page (this simply depends on how you set the site up). Alternatively, your customer can click the *'Checkout'* button and place the order on the Cart (Basket) page.

**Your Shopping Basket**

| Remove Product(s) | | Qty. | Total |
|---|---|---|---|
| | **Parrot MKi9000 Bluetooth Car Kit**<br>*- Vehicle & Radio Audi : TT 2006-On with Chorus Radios* | 1 | £117.60 |
| | | Sub-Total: | £117.60 |

Continue Shopping — Checkout

*Traditional/Standard Shopping Cart (Basket) Page*

**New Cart Process:** When your prospect *'adds product to cart'* they stay on the product page. They are then presented with a confirmation (pop-up) displaying the cart activity. They are not automatically taken to the cart page as in the Standard Cart Process. The cart page still exists, but you only go there if you click the *'View Cart'* or *'Basket'* link.

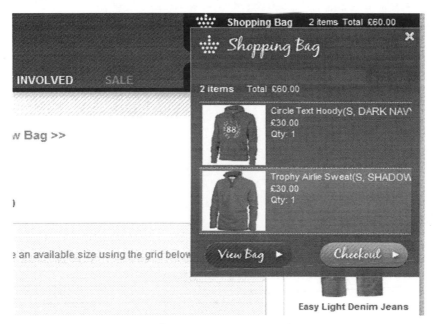

*Newer Type Shopping Cart (Basket) Feature*

# 4) Conversion.

Usability and Conversion go hand in hand. Without great usability your website conversion rate will suck. Conversion is the process of converting a prospect into a customer. A conversion equals a sale.

When you first launch your website, it will not be firing on all cylinders. There is no way you'll get it converting at the optimum visitor-to-sales conversion rate from the outset, until you analyze user data - and this can only be carried out once you actually have enough traffic to gather usable data. Only when you consistently get at least 30–50 people a day on our website will you have enough metrics to judge and get actual results. The more visitors per day, the more accurate the data will be.

However working on a website that is growing and not yet at its peak is not a problem. If you recall the *'You Don't Have To Get It Right, You Just Have to Get it Going'* quote from earlier in the book, then you'll realize there will always be room for improvement, and increases in your conversion rate. ***Analyzing user data is detailed in Element 15) 'Analytics & Reports'.***

*'Use These Critical Conversion Tips On Your Website Today and Immediately Boost Profits... Or Use When You Have Enough User Data!'*

87

# Marketing Costs vs. Conversion Increases.

**Should you be spending money on marketing if your conversion rate is poor?** You can and should, but then at least pause when you get enough data to analyze and refine, as mentioned above. In Step 1 (Traffic > Conversion > Relationships), we touched on the results attainable if you continue to refine your website over its life cycle. This can increase conversion rates from 1% to 4% overnight. Moreover, by doing so, if you sell one product per day at $100, then overnight after making subtle design and navigational changes you could be taking $400 without spending another cent on marketing.

E-commerce websites characteristically have two main resistance points. This ultimately means visitors to your website will stay and buy your products, or they will leave faster than they arrived.

**Resistance Point 1:** The moment a prospect enters your website.

As you approximately have 5–7 seconds to capture your visitor's attention, you need to get them interested in what you have to offer and make them stick to your website. They will either click to another page, buy your product or leave. If they leave on the page they enter on, this affects your visitor-to-sales conversion rate and bounce rate. Resistance Point One can come from any design or layout element: poor colors, images, text (headlines & descriptions), buttons (shape, color, and text), badly worded links, poor navigation, a design that's too busy, price. Remember, this is primarily a subconscious decision.

The average conversion rate on an e-commerce website is less than 1%. Less than one in every one hundred visitors to the average e-commerce site will leave without buying a product. Bounce Rate as we will discuss later in element *14) 'Analytics'* section is the percentage of people that enter your website on a specific page, and leave from the same page without clicking to another page—they see only a single page before leaving.

**Resistance Point 2:** Any Step of Your Website Checkout Process.

A prospect has landed on your website, and they are interested in your products. They *'add to cart',* and enter your checkout process. This is the next critical zone where prospects tend to drop-out! Average dropped shopping cart percentages (also known as cart abandonment rates) are in the 80% plus range. This is when a would-be-customer leaves your cart checkout process and your website without buying. For every one hundred people entering the checkout process, only twenty or less on average will complete their order.

For every additional step (or page) you have in your checkout process, you potentially lose more and more would-be customers. We will address this in section 5), *'Checkout'.* There may obviously be more areas of your website that create resistance to your prospects, but it is of critical importance to get these two points right.

*Usability and converting traffic comes down to **'Keep it Simple!'***

# 5) Checkout.

Continuing from section 4) Conversion, a short and smooth checkout process is crucial for maximizing orders. As we now know, *Cart Abandonment* is a huge problem for e-commerce websites. The need to eliminate checkout resistance and consequently reduce cart abandonment rates is of prime importance, and this alone can mean the difference between an extra $10K and $100K plus in sales per month.

**Reduce Checkout Resistance.**

We need a fast checkout process that is seamless with as few as steps as possible and little or no resistance. It has to be clean and simple with no distractions, so I recommend removing your left and right menus—just like Amazon do—and keep the text to a minimum and make it very succinct with clear and basic instructions of what you want the customer to do.

Amazon actually go one step further and remove the header navigation too with only a small *'Go to the Amazon.com home page (without completing your order)'* link at the bottom of their final Order Review page. This is taking their checkout process to the next level; its laser focused but could be one step too far for a small business e-commerce website. Run tests and you will know which is best.

Display help notifications on small pop-ups—visible when a would-be customer places the cursor to hover over an *'info link'*—where required, assisting your shoppers so the whole checkout process is seamless and self-explanatory. Any detailed *'how to order guides'* will go in your help or customer support area. Your prospects are emotionally charged during a checkout phase and are not thinking logically, so do not make them think too much or your sale could be lost.

**In summary:** During the checkout process do not give prospects too many options and definitely do NOT give them a checkout degree course!

## Checkout Breadcrumbs:

Using a breadcrumb trail in your checkout process is important as it shows your prospects exactly where they are in the checkout process and how many steps are left to order completion. This guide is by way of links, small image icons or both and can help reduce cart and checkout abandonments.

*4 Checkout Breadcrumb Trail Examples*

## Checkout Page Security Requisites.

Display clear yet subtle security and credit card logos, and maybe a small padlock or security image in the checkout process. These will build trust and familiarity. You will need a secure checkout—this is mandatory—and your web developer or hosting company will provide the Secure Socket Layer (SSL). See an example verification image below of an SSL enabled website.

Using an SSL will 100% secure your website checkout area and an 's' will appear in your domain name (as in 'https://...', instead of just 'http://...') when in the checkout. In addition, an image of a padlock will appear in your visitors' browser.

**Note:** You should NOT make the whole website secure, as it will slow the load speed down massively and is unnecessary. Only secure your checkout.

*Unsecure (Top Image) and Secure URL's - Notice the https (Bottom Image)*

*A Secure Socket Layer (SSL) Enabled Website, Displaying SSL Certificate*

## Coupon/Discount Voucher Code Box.

If you have a Coupon or Discount Voucher Code box in your checkout area, and you are not currently running discount promotions, then disable it. Customers are fickle and easily distracted. Many will leave your checkout page and go hunting for money off coupon codes—and the problem is that many would-be-customers will never return to complete their order.

So (see section 14 *'Marketing Elements'*) get your web developer to add the facility to disable this box from the back-end admin, as and when required. If you are not running any coupon code (money-off) promotions then turn the box off in the checkout: make it disappear until you need it.

| 2. Do you have a promotion/catalogue code? | | |
|---|---|---|
| Enter your promotion code and then click 'update': | | UPDATE |

*Example Discount Coupon/Voucher Code Box As Found In Checkout*

## Create Account.

Another potential problem is if you ask people to *'sign up'* or *'create account'* in your checkout area: this can greatly increase cart abandonment rates. The majority of people do not like to sign up or create an account when buying. Therefore, you can subtly word this so that your prospects believe they are simply *'entering their billing details'* or *'shipping details'* and this eliminates the enemy of resistance. Your prospect is actually creating an account by giving you their details, but you do not need to advertise the fact. Larger and more reputable companies such as Amazon—having more brand awareness—can explicitly ask you to create an account with fewer cart dropouts.

*A Typical 'Create Account' Form - This Is How NOT to Word Your Checkout*

**New Customer**

I am a new customer.

By creating an account at 'sitename' you will be able to shop faster, be up to date on an orders status, and keep track of the orders you have previously made.

▶ Continue

**Returning Customer**

I am a returning customer.

E-Mail Address:

Password:

Password forgotten? Click here.

⟳ Sign In

*Account Set-Up Process*

## Amazon.com Express Checkout.

At the time of writing Amazon.com has recently launched *'Pay Phrase'*, a simple way to verify your account to speed up purchasing. You set up a unique phrase like *'Web Warrior'* and select a 4-digit PIN. This is linked to your Amazon account, which is pre-loaded with your credit card and shipping address. Whether it actually speeds up purchasing though, is another question.

# Setting Up Checkout Funnel Goals to Monitor Cart Abandonment.

Many website checkout areas and processes are too complex, time consuming and have up to seven different pages. If you monitor your website stats—by setting up Goals in Google's free Analytics software—you will see where people drop out and at which step in the checkout process.

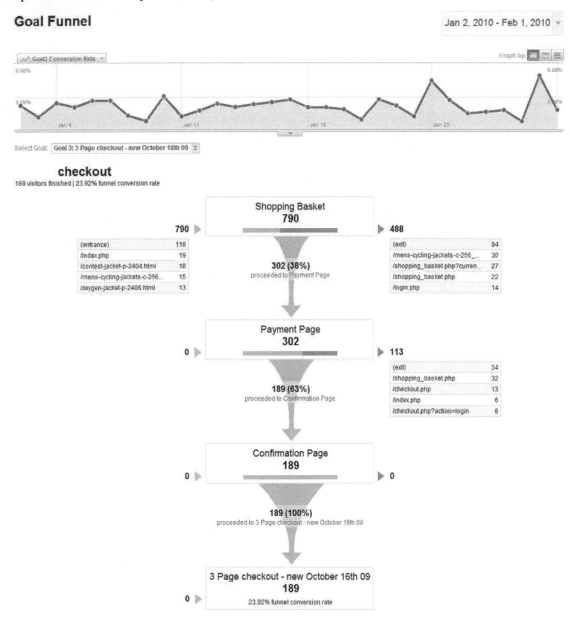

*Traditional Checkout Using Google Analytics Goals and Showing Cart (Basket) Abandonment Rates (Dropped Baskets) At Each Stage of the Checkout Process*

### What Creates Checkout Resistance?

- Slow loading speed

- Too many steps, too many pages, too many options, too many distractions

- Too confusing or too busy

- Using the words *'Create Account'* can be a problem depending on product and customer type.

- Broken forms or fields (needs testing in different browsers and platforms such as Internet Explorer, Firefox, Google Chrome, Safari, Windows & Apple Mac)

- Discount Code Box Can entice potential customers to leave the site to look for discount codes

- Not secure (lack of SSL certificate, no *'s'* in the https in URL [Web Address] & no padlock symbol in browser)

- Poor trust due to no visible security logos or accreditations such as MasterCard, Visa, PayPal, Bank Logos, Shopping Safe accreditations like BBB (US), McAfee Secure or FSB & ISIS in the UK

- Button color, shape & wording

## Cart & Checkout Buttons.

The color, shape and wording used on buttons can play a huge part in conversion rates. Imagine a big square-edged button, saying *'BUY NOW'* in a bright red color. Contrast this with a round edged button, in blue saying *'Add to Cart'*. In testing, you will find different emotional responses evoked between the two buttons, affecting sales.

This is not only about button characteristics but also depends on your product and positioning, so use appropriate button elements. Not only in your product, cart and checkout pages, but site-wide (across the whole website) as well, consider your button shape, color and wording.

*Random Shopping Cart Buttons. What Emotions Do These Evoke In You?*

## The 1–Page Checkout Model.

In 2005 my team and I spent a lot of time analyzing the checkout process on my websites, monitoring the cart-abandonment rates and testing various checkout set-ups, using split testing and multivariate testing. This is the process of using two or more different checkout concepts and modifying on-page elements, randomly showing each one to customers and measuring the results. You then select the best performing setup, modify further until you reach your desired conversion rate, and then use it permanently on the live site. Incidentally, this can be applied to almost any area of your website, from buttons to pages—more on split and multivariate testing in Step 4.

As a result, we designed and built a pioneering 1–page checkout. This new and exclusive checkout page immediately follows the cart (shopping) basket page and contains all user forms on the one page in five simple steps. I have various different layouts on this model and all undergo thorough testing to ensure they improve conversion rates before permanent use on the live site.

### Will This Checkout Format Improve Conversions On All Websites?

The simple answer is that you need to test! Using a 1–page checkout is definitely not mandatory, but testing is. In a perfect scenario, you would run split testing on your normal checkout versus the new one page checkout and measure the results. Split testing would serve up both checkouts randomly and you pick the one that converts more sales.

### The 1 Page Checkout Form & 5 Simple Step Process for Customer:

1) Step 1: Billing Details

2) Step 2: Shipping Details

3) Step 3: Shipping Option

4) Step 4: Payment Method

5) Step 5: Create Password

6) Order Preview Box with simple overview of the items being paid for

7) Click 'Confirm Order' Button

**Note:** The text at the side of password in brackets disguises a 'sign up to account' process. It says something like 'A password allows you to view your orders, print invoices, and make address changes, action returns and place future orders faster'.

Each step on the checkout page is accompanied by a small *'Info'* link, which gives you a small pop up with information assistance when you hover over it.

**Note:** For reference, I detailed the *'Create Password'* text above as people get suspicious about creating accounts and passwords as discussed earlier.

*Design Example of a Seamless 1 Page Checkout (Taken from Many Design Variants). All Variants Need Split-Testing Before Using Permanently.*

## Order Confirmation Page.

Once an order has been placed on your website, your customer will be presented with the *'Order Confirmation Page'* (also known as Order Success Page). This mainly says *'Thanks for your order!'* However, this page can be greatly improved and utilized for much more.

When a customer has just ordered they have endorphins rushing around their bodies. This is the ideal opportunity to offer them something else, as they are highly responsive. Put more products in front of them now.

### *Order Confirmation Page Tips:*

* Say *'Thank you'* to your customer. Explain their invoice will be emailed to them and give expected shipping times and that multiple items may be delivered at separate times if one is out of stock

* Ask them to check their Spam folder if they fail to receive your email invoice. This will cut down on support requests

* You can offer a Newsletter Sign Up or RSS

* If you have multiple websites, place banners or links to your other websites here

* Offer related and recommended products

* Place Google Adsense (to make money on the exit click)

* Promote other peoples products and services (affiliate links) where available

## Example 1: Order Confirmation Page (screen shot below) using these features:

1) Thanks for Your Order message:

**Thank you for your order!**

We will send you an e-mail confirmation shortly.

**Note:** If you have ordered several items, we may send them to you in separate packages to give you the fastest service. This will not affect your shipping charges.

**Note:** Please await receipt of our *Order Dispatch email* prior to arranging an installation or booking time off work. This will prevent any unnecessary inconvenience. Thanks for your cooperation.

**Please Note:** If you fail to receive an email Order Invoice from us in your Inbox, please check the following folders in your email software: Junk, Spam, Deleted Items, Bulk or similar folders.

2) *'Manage Your Account'* links

3) Banners promoting related websites

4) Email newsletter opt-in

5) Continue Shopping Button linking to Home Page

6) Customer Survey

***Example 1: Order Confirmation Page***

## Example 2: Order Confirmation Page (screen shot below) using these features:

1) Thanks for Your Order message:

**Thank you for your order!**

We will send you an e-mail confirmation shortly.

**Note:** If you have ordered several items, we may send them to you in separate packages to give you the fastest service. This will not affect your shipping charges.

**Note:** Please await receipt of our *Order Dispatch email* prior to arranging an installation or booking time off work. This will prevent any unnecessary inconvenience. Thanks for your cooperation.

**Please Note**: If you fail to receive an email Order Invoice from us in your Inbox please check the following folders in your email software: Junk, Spam, Deleted Items, Bulk or similar folders.

2) RSS Subscribe Option

Subscribe to the In Car iPod RSS feed

Subscribe now to the In Car iPod RSS feed in 1 easy click and get news, product reviews, special offers and updates. Click the orange RSS tag and you'll get the RSS feed straight to the RSS reader of your choice, or by email as and when we release it.

3) Manage Your Account Links

• Your order has been successfully processed!

• You can view your order history by going to '*My Account*' page and by clicking on '*History*'

• If you have any questions regarding your order please '*Contact Us*'

4) Recommended Products: Customers who bought the item(s) in your order also bought

5) Banner advertising other product or service

6) You may be interested in these related websites

7) Large Graphic Banner advertising new (cross sell) products

8) Newsletter opt-in

9) '*Continue Shopping*' button that takes them back to Home Page

10) Site links

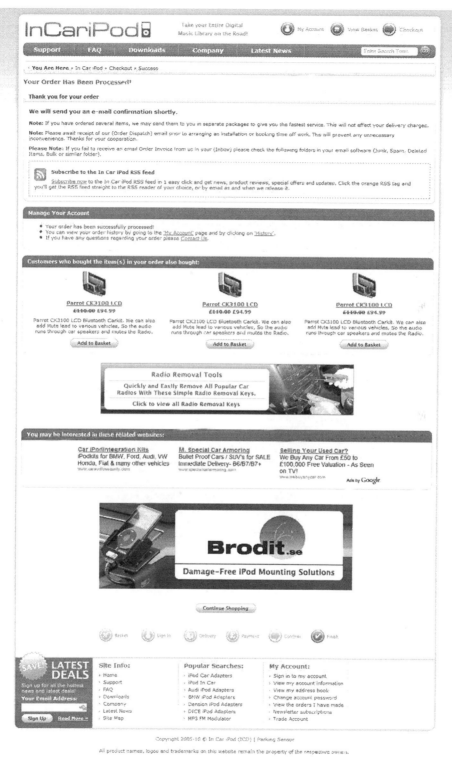

**Example 2: Order Confirmation Page**

# 6) Taking Payments.

Accepting credit and debit cards is mandatory for E-commerce websites. This method is fast and efficient for you and your customers and with the introduction of cash-balance credit cards, practically anyone has access to a credit card to use as payment.

In addition to accepting credit and debit cards, you also have the option to accept payment by phone, fax, mail and bank transfer, but the majority will pay online or by phone using a credit card. My recommendation is to accept credit and debit cards and bank transfer, removing unnecessary payment options. Keep the process simple and clinical.

My latest data shows approximately 80% of customers order online and 20% order by phone. When customers pay by phone you can (a) run an order through an online *'virtual terminal'*—that your card payment processing company provides you with—or (b) you can just process the order through the website as customers do. Either way is fully secure.

There are hundreds of companies offering online payments and there are two main models.

## 1. Payment Service Provider.

Worldpay, PayPal or Google offer a fully integrated payment system. They not only (a) encrypt the transaction making it 100% secure once the data leaves your website, but also (b) handle and process the payments.

## 2. Payment Gateway and Acquiring Bank.

Like the above but using two different companies to handle each of the two processes separately. Both companies communicate seamlessly to ensure the transaction is encrypted and secure. Some companies offer both solutions (1 & 2) so please check when you get quotations.

***Typical & Simplified Customer Order Process:***

**Step 1:** Customer orders on your website >

**Step 2:** Payment gateway securely passes transaction details to bank >

**Step 3:** Bank approves and completes the transaction >

**Step 4:** You and your customer both get *'order confirmation'* on screen and by email.

WorldPay provides an international solution that can be used for the US market, for the UK market, and so on. Other solutions may be oriented to certain countries in particular, such as Streamline for the UK. I recommend SagePay as the Payment

Gateway and Streamline (RBS) as the acquiring bank for UK based customers.

Basic fees payable are: setup, transaction fees per sale such as 2% of the transaction value and a monthly minimum limit. Be wary of any other 'stealth fees' such as refund charges.

### Start With These Merchant Account Providers from the Hundreds Available:

- Google Checkout: www.googlecheckout.com
- PayPal: www.paypal.com
- WorldPay: www.worldpay.com
- SagePay: www.sagepay.com
- Streamline: www.streamline.com
- The 3rd Man: www.the3rdman.co.uk

## HOT TIP

*When applying for your merchant account you will be asked to forecast your annual turnover. The higher your turnover generally the lower your transaction fees will be so don't be too conservative here because if you can save 0.25% to .5% per transaction this will equate to quite a saving over 12 months. Also negotiate these fees every 6 months as sales grow.*

## Multiple Currencies.

If you accept orders from other countries consider accepting payments in your customers' currency. The top 3 online are Dollar, Euro and Pound Sterling. There are 2 ways to do this:

1) Add a currency module to your e-commerce software–with currency selection buttons on your site–that gives site users the option to click a link that changes all prices on the site in to their chosen currency. When they order the currency will show as the site default currency on the payment processors payment page and on their credit card statement (but typically converted into their own currency).

Currency £ / € / $

*Simple Currency Button Example (With Various Currency Selection Options) to Display On a Website - Attracting International Customer Transactions*

2) In addition to the above for on-site viewing, you can also accept the payment in their chosen currency. When a customer orders they will pay in their own currency: this will show on the payment processor's payment page and on their credit card statement. This option is more expensive and you will need a separate merchant number for each currency that you accept: so if you accept Dollar, Euro and GBP then this will triple the application costs.

***Integration Options for Payment Gateway and Acquiring Bank:***

There are essentially 3 ways to integrate this system with your website and each one offers a flexible solution. The terms I use may change with each Payment Gateway company.

# 1) Form

Form integration is the quickest way to start processing online payments. It can take as little as 20 minutes to set up and is by far the easiest way to integrate with your payment gateway.

**This is good if...**

- You are unable, or do not wish, to maintain your own secure web servers and have chosen instead to have them managed by a third party hosting company

- Your website is run from a shared system with the same web server delivering many different web sites. In these circumstances, an individual company has very limited abilities to install anything more than simple HTML pages and script files, and cannot normally install items outside their own user area (especially if this involves components that will affect the entire server)

- You do not wish for any sensitive information to be collected or stored on your site. This removes the need for you to maintain highly secure encrypted databases, obtain digital certificates and invest in high-level PCI DSS compliance

***Comments:*** This is the more popular and well known option but has limitations. The customer is taken from your checkout page across to the payment gateway that may be branded as PayPal, SagePay, Worldpay with your logo on there too if required. If you've ever bought online and been taken off the site to process your order and then returned back to the site post order, then you used *'Form'*.

# 2) Server

Server integration is recommended to merchants who want to run order & transaction reports on their own servers, but don't want to invest in their own digital certificate or collect credit card details on their own website.

- Database compatibility: Server integration offers you a more advanced database compatibility, meaning you can store more information about the transaction such as the amount, the products selected, the shopper's contact details and the result of the authorization supplied by your payment provider

– Customization: The payment pages are fully customizable. Server integration also comes with in-Frame technology, where your secure payment fields are framed by your branding, meaning your customer doesn't even move from your URL. This instantly reduces the need for high-level PCI DSS compliance and doesn't compromise your customers' shopping experience on your site

**Comments:** I've never processed transactions in my office manually. But if you have a card machine or terminal in your office this will be the option for you giving you control of the transaction and refund process.

**Note:** Server integration is compatible with many shopping carts and e-commerce platforms; however some off-the-shelf shopping carts can only be used in conjunction with Form integration. Check with your shopping cart provider.

## 3) Direct

Direct integration is designed to enable you to take card details on your own secure servers and pass them across to Sage Pay (for example) for authorization and secure storage in a server-to-server session that does not involve redirecting the shopper to your payment providers' payment pages.

– It is the method by which you pass the data to your payment gateway, not the method by which you collect it, meaning you have complete control over the look and feel of your payment pages

– Your customer never leaves your site and they do not necessarily know your payment provider is authorizing the transaction on your behalf. In practice however many vendors choose to tell their shoppers as a way of reassuring them about card security

– It is ideal for large companies with existing back office payment software, such as a call center that wants to integrate their payment system and manage the whole of the payment process internally

**Comments:** Direct is my preferred option as all transactions appear to happen on your website and the customer appears to never leave your website alleviating any issues of confusion or risk. It's slick, seamless, integrated and fast. Plus you can make it look exactly how you want it to look.

## Two Order Processing Options:

When choosing a method of accepting credit and debit cards and the processing of these payments, you essentially have two choices: real-time processing and deferred processing.

1) **Real-Time Order Processing:** Means the credit card and all security checks are approved automatically without your intervention in real time. The main negatives to this method are: if you subsequently see something suspicious about the order and think that it may be fraud, you will have to refund the order and lose the initial transaction fee. In the same way, if a customer rings up and cancels after placing an order, you will again lose the transaction fee

2) **Deferred Order Processing:** Means the order is approved as above, but only a shadow payment for the order value is placed on the customer's card, used for the order. The order details are also sent to your payment admin area, so you as the merchant have a set period of time—often 30 days—to accept and process, or decline the order. The positives of this are that you have time to run your own security checks, or contact the customer with any questions, such as shipping related queries or if an item is out of stock. This can save you the transaction fee if you subsequently choose to decline the order

## Fraud Prevention.

Ask your future payment service provider what fraud prevention features and services they offer. The majority now offer these three Cardholder Not Present (CNP) fraud prevention services as standard. There is also the possibility to set bespoke fraud '*Rule Sets*'. This allows you to tailor your desired and specific anti-fraud measures on your website, giving you optimal flexibility and peace of mind.

1) **AVS:** Address Verification System is a method used to verify the identity of the person claiming to own the credit card who is ordering on your website. It works by matching the data entered into your website '*Billing*' order form with the address on file at the credit card company

2) **Card Verification Code:** Also known as CVV, CV2, CVVC, CVC amongst others, this is the last 3-digit number on the back of the credit or debit card. If a fraudster has the physical stolen credit card then he or she will have this number also, so other security is required

3) **3D Secure:** Is a technical standard created by **'Visa (Verified by Visa)'** and **'MasterCard (MasterCard SecureCode)'** to further secure CNP (Cardholder Not Present) transactions over the Internet. New customers, who have not yet used the 3D facility on their card, will set up a password or pass code when they first try to pay on a 3D secure activated website. Then for subsequent online orders, they will simply provide the password or code chosen on the 3D page. This service is provided to you as a merchant through your payment provider as a bolt-on service for your website (not mandatory) and has pros and cons

**3D Positives:** it's water tight, unless the fraudster has found out your security pass. Also, be aware some customers may only buy from a 3D secure website.

**3D Negatives:** it adds resistance to your checkout process involving an extra step in the order process that genuine customers must go through. On the other hand, if a fraudster does get hold of the password of the stolen card he or she is using, this will result in a spend-fest until the card is registered as *'stolen'* by the real card owner

4) **Bespoke Rule Sets:** I use SagePay as my payment gateway provider in conjunction with Streamline (RBS) the acquiring bank. SagePay offer an additional fraud screening service provided by *'The 3<sup>rd</sup> Man'*: this gives you a fraud potential rating for each order, based on the transaction details. These bespoke *'Rule Sets'* give you the ability as a merchant to determine what extra level of security you feel your website needs. In addition, this flexibility is very useful, as some product markets will have more fraud attempts than others. Some countries will also produce more fraud attempts than other countries, Nigeria being one hot spot for fraud attempts.

*\*Please check with your payment provider to see if they offer similar anti-fraud services.*

## MasterCard SecureCode.

MasterCard SecureCode is a simple and secure way to pay at thousands of online stores. A private code known only to you and your bank, your SecureCode enhances your existing MasterCard account by protecting you against unauthorized use of your card when shopping online at participating online retailers.

- MasterCard SecureCode: www.mastercard.com/securecode

## Verified by Visa.

Verified by Visa protects consumers by requiring a password during online purchases, helping ensure no one else can use their Visa card online. Verified by Visa also protects merchants from fraud-related chargebacks on all Visa personal debit and credit card transactions, even when processing transactions from non-participating issuers.

- VerifiedByVisa: www.visa.com/verifiedbyvisa

### HOT TIP

*For UK Customers: If you sign up for an FSB (Federation of Small Business) account, you are eligible for a discount on Streamline transaction fees. FSB membership also gives UK based companies insurance, protecting you against tax investigations. Contact them for more info: www.FSB.org.uk*

# 7) Product Pages.

How you present the products is crucial for a successful e-commerce website. Look at the big name e-commerce websites such as iHerb.com, Amazon.com, Crutchfield.com, GAP.com, JohnLewis.com, FatFace.com for ideas. See how their product information is laid out on the page in ways that are structured and presented with clarity so you can find items quickly and intuitively.

***Elements of a Successful Product Layout Template:***

- Product name in bold type using product keywords: this generates an H1 tag for SEO – more on this in 8) below

- Short description placed underneath the product name: this has an H2 tag

- Image to the left of the center container with the ability to *'View Larger Image',* to view more related images (thumbnails will sit underneath main image), or an option to magnify any area of main image

- Use alt text on images

- Add to Cart (Add to Basket) box or its elements to right of image: RRP, your price, % saving, quantity, size, color options, warranty, availability, Add to Cart button, etc.

- Position the product description, with heading underneath the main image and Add to Cart box. Utilize supplementary images to enhance the description

- Bulleted feature list with heading positioned underneath the main product description

- Any further information positioned below, such as related information or Technical Info

- Detail any shipping, print this page, warranty, email a friend, social bookmarks, supplementary but essential info either below the images and above the description or below the description box (as long as the page is not so long that readers get lost)

## Attributes.

You will need to decide how many products you will be selling, the way they are laid out on the page, and what fields, attributes and options you will need per product. Attributes such as size, color and quantity all need to be factored in and positioned accordingly.

**Parking Dynamics PD1 Parking Sensor**

Universal Front & Rear Parking Sensors - No Holes Universal Parking Sensor

*universal*

PD1 Rear or PD1 Vision Rear Option

RRP: £119.99
Your Price: £79.97
You Save: £40.02 (33%)
Warranty: 2 Years

Select Front or Rear Sensor Option:

PD1-Rear (£79.97)

Quantity: 1   Add to Basket

In Stock. Order in the next 50 hours, 14 minutes
For guaranteed delivery on Tuesday

1, 2, 3+ Click Here For Multi-Buy Discounts

| Product Details | Product Info | Customer Tools | Services |
|---|---|---|---|
| View Description | View Installation | Email Page | Delivery Charges |
| View Features | Read Customer Reviews | Print this page | 30 Day Money Back |

*Example Showing How to Display Many Attributes and Key On-Site (On-Page)
SEO Attributes In a Small Compact Area*

## Images.

Include the basics like web-ready and compressed images so they load fast. Use high quality images for the main image, thumbnails (the small image preview) or additional images, and for the '*view larger image*' option.

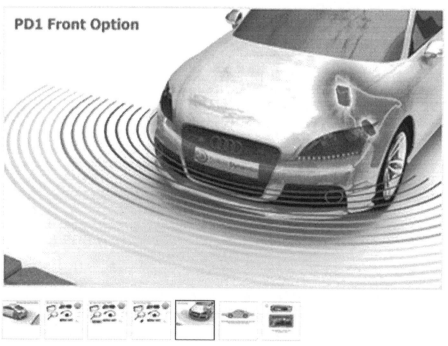

PD1 Front Option

*Thumbnail Preview Images - Appearing Large In Main Image On Hover*

*View Larger Image With Clear 'Close Window' Button*

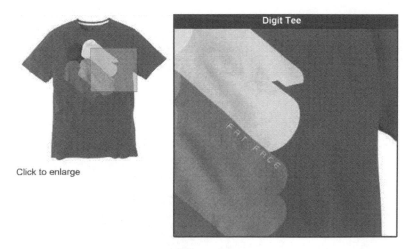

*Magnify (Zoom) Main Image*

## Tabbed Layout.

A good option is to have the description, features, and shipping information in tabbed boxes in the same page location as the main description. This keeps the page short and compact. This just depends on your SEO aspirations and desired page layout.

- See www.fatface.com (for an example of this tabbed product layout - image below)
- Or checkout www.crutchfield.com (who are great at tabbed layouts)

*Tabbed Product Layout*

## Product Descriptions.

Use a benefit-oriented headline to capture the attention of your visitor when they arrive on your page. They may get to this page directly from Google. A H2 tag attached to this headline always helps for SEO. Use well-written descriptions promoting benefits and then list features using bullet points, in this order. If a customer can say *'So What?'* to your description copy then introduce more benefits and remove features from this section, dropping them into the bullet point feature list below. Add video where required as this enables the buyer to use more of their five senses to make a positive buying decision.

## Long Copy vs. Short Copy.

There is a debate in marketing circles: do you write short copy or long copy? E-commerce and direct response are two very different animals in my opinion, but you can use direct response elements on an e-commerce website. However, this has to work in synergy without cheapening the positioning, and that is the big challenge.

People who succumb to out and out direct response are generally vulnerable and somewhat naive, which is why some Internet Marketing Gurus and Get Rich Quick businesses make a bundle of cash—because they manipulate as opposed to persuade—through their words, targeting gullible people.

E-commerce customers are a different breed in many respects. They will actually be looking for your products, so the use of direct response needs to be subtle and woven in with your typical e-commerce layout. Do you recall the key advice earlier in this book - *'Fast, Functional & Familiar'?*

- See this page for a great product layout with lots of keyword rich content: www. parkingdynamics.co.uk/Universal-Sensors/Parking-Dynamics-PD1/Parking-Dynamics-PD1-Parking-Sensor

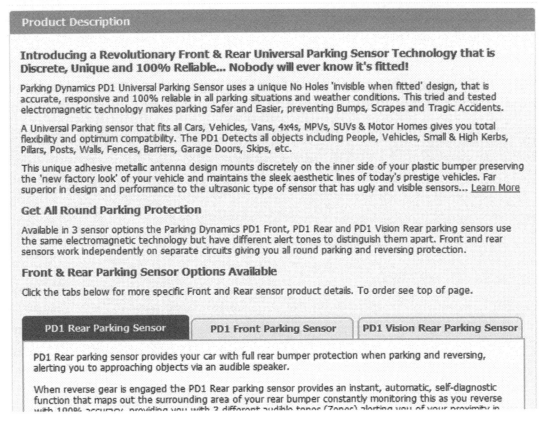

*Example of Captive Headline (H1 Tag) and Long Description Loaded With Keywords and Key Phrases - Long Copy On an E-commerce Website*

## Product Pages Resource Information.

It's a good idea to display and link to key information your prospects or customers may need to make a buying decision. Not answering their required questions and your customers could leave them frustrated. They might then either leave your website or leave your product page looking for specific answers—and never return.

*Possible Resource Items or Links to These Items:*

- Print Page, Email Page, Bookmark Page
- Shipping Details (Options, Prices, Delivery Times)

- Product Warranties & Money Back Guarantees
- Customer Reviews, Product Comparison

***Product Resource Box Examples: Providing Key Information & Answering Key Questions On the Product Page Itself (Eliminating Need to Have to Leave the Product Page)***

## Add to Cart Box.

This box or alternatively these elements positioned around your *'Add to Cart'* button will contain all the essential information required for your prospect to be comfortable enough to add your products to their shopping cart. Items required here are: price, attributes, options, quantity, shipping times, stock availability, brand of product. The best position for this box is to the right of the main product image, because people read from the left. The Add to Cart button (or *'Add to Basket'* - in the UK), will sit underneath the price and other options because people also read from top to bottom.

***4 Add to Cart (Add to Basket) Box Examples With Key Info In Each***

### *Add to Cart (Add to Basket) Box Elements Could Include:*

- Clear Prices, including Marked Down Recommended Retail Prices (RRP's) with % off

- Attributes: Color, Size, Quantity
- Stock Levels & Availability of Product
- Warranty
- Money Back Guarantee
- Security Features and Guarantees
- Discounts for Large or Bulk Orders
- Price Matching Option if You Offer this
- Customer Reviews

All of the above areas give the customer the appropriate details required to make a buying decision.

# 8) On-Site (On-Page) SEO (Search Engine Optimization).

On-Site SEO also known as On-Page SEO is the process and skill set of engineering your website with SEO techniques exclusive to your website pages, and not techniques that are used off of and external from your website (Off-Site SEO or Off-Page SEO).

Using super-charged SEO modules and 'White Hat' strategies on your e-commerce website is your secret weapon. This builds a solid SEO foundation to get you ranked high in Google in the shortest space of time, and as a bonus these modules come with the initial website build.

*White Hat simply means ethical and in-line with Google's recommended practices.*

I have had websites attain number 1 ranking in Google with on-site SEO only (no off-site SEO at all), and this costs nothing other than a bit of time updating the key SEO tags as you grow. I highly recommend you get this groundwork right from the outset to give you an SEO advantage now and into the future.

80% of search engine users use Google. I recommend reading Google Webmaster Guidelines to ensure you keep it legal and so Google loves your website. Many SEO guys are fighting against and trying to trick Google, but that's simply not required.

- Google Webmaster Guidelines: www.google.com/support/webmasters

***Ask Your Web Developer to Give You These Features and Options As a Minimum:***

- Meta Page Titles (Title Tag) with data extraction and population from the name field in each product (also manually editable to further supercharge SEO results)

- Meta Description
- Meta Keywords
- H1 Tags automatically assigned to Name Field on Product Page
- H2 Tags automatically assigned to Short Description Field on Product Page
- H1 Tags automatically assigned to Info Page Header Title
- H2 Tags automatically assigned to Product Headline
- Load text first in the center container
- Make your website header smaller in height than the norm so that more text can fit on the page and *'above the fold'* (on the screen before you have to scroll to see the full page)

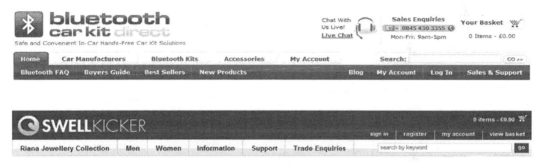

*2 Examples of Well Balanced Header Heights, Enabling More Page Content to Be Seen Above The Fold (Without Scrolling Down the Page)*

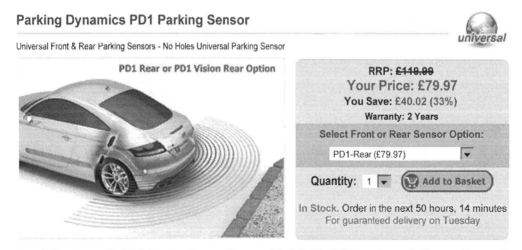

*On-Site (On-Page) SEO In Action - Name Field (Bold Text) and Short Description Fields Above the Main Product Image*

- **Parking Dynamics PD1 Parking Sensor** = Name Field (a H1 Tag) and can be automated to display all of this content or just part, as the Page Title
- **Universal Front & Rear Parking Sensors – No Holes Universal Parking Sensor** = Short Description Field (a H2 Tag)

## SEO On-Page Factors Overview:

### *Page Title (Title Tag).*

This is the bar at the top of your browser window when you're on a website. It's also the first thing Google reads on your page when indexing it. A good page title (also known as the Title Tag) is critical in order to rank well in Google. All things being equal, the page (website) with the best matched page title ranks the highest. You have approx 62–68 characters to use in your page titles. Consult with Google for its latest page title character count. It is very important to point out that each page title on your website has to be unique.

**Page Title Example 1:** Cure My Anxiety | Anxiety Help | Reduce Stress Now

**Page Title Example 2:** Welcome to Cure My Anxiety – Learn to Reduce Stress Now

**Note:** Stop words (and, of, in, is, it, or, to etc.) are not read by Google in the page title, so limit the use of these.

As your page title is displayed in the Google search results, it has to be engineered for Google and captivating for Google searchers—your prospects—to get them to click the link and enter your website.

### *Two Examples of Page Titles:*

**Natural Anxiety Cure** | Panic Treatment | Self Help With Anxiety
Help and Advice in Recovering from Panic and **Anxiety** Attacks by ex-sufferer Paul David. You'll find valuable information including symptoms and causes of ...

Natural Anxiety Cure | Panic Treatment | Self Help With Anxiety Attacks - Mozilla Firefox

*Page Title (Title Tag) As Seen In Search Engine Result When Searching for a Keyword (Top Image) and As Seen At Top of Browser When On Website*

## Meta Description.

Not actually visible on your website, but hidden in the code and is used by Google to determine the content of each page on your site. Google lists this below your page title in the Google search results so make it read well. Optimum is approximately 14–16 words or 160 characters. See example of a Meta Description text in the top image just above. This sits below the blue (bold) Page Title link.

## Meta Keywords.

My recommendation is to use 5–6 keywords per page in this box as your competitors can steal your keywords if you give away too many. Google doesn't currently use this tag but the other search engines do.

## Header Tags.

Known as H1, H2, H3. These tags are used to help the search engines see the important headings on your page. Only H1 and H2 really have any value now so you need to use these as bold headings in your copy, as in menu headings, menu category headings, on page headings. Use only one H1 tag per page, as your page headline or heading (on each page of your site). Use H2 tags on your other headings.

## Image Alt Text.

When you hover on an image on a website, you'll often see a piece of text appear; this is Alternative Text or Alt Text for short. Not used so much by Google now but is very useful information to visitors to your webpage, if an image does not load in certain browsers. Essential for site users with visual impairment.

## PageRank.

PageRank is one of the methods Google uses to determine a page's relevance or importance, in addition to Link Popularity and Link Reputation. Incidentally, Google ranks pages and not websites, so each page on your website is ranked on its own merits. Google PageRank is on a scale of 1–10. 1 being a new website, 10 being Google. The more backlinks your website has (links pointing to your site) the more PageRank your website will accumulate.

### PageRank Essentially Does Two Things:

1) Indicates whether Google considers you to be an authority website

2) Indicates how often Google will send its spiders (robots) to index your site pages. The higher the PageRank, the more often your site is indexed

When building a website it is essential to build the structure of the site, so PageRank can flow around easily without resistance, and get down to the deepest product pages, and then link back up to the home page. Using the *'No Follow'* attribute can distribute PageRank effectively around your site.

## Duplicate Content.

Google does not like duplicate content and will not rank duplicate pages found on the same website. Each URL and page title has to be unique. It is fine if you happen to sell the same product but from different manufactures—such as an iPod Car Kit for all manufactures A to Z (Alfa Romeo to Volkswagen)—you just need a unique URL, Page Title, Headline (H1) and (H2's) by replacing the manufacture keyword site-wide. Remember also—do not plagiarize content from other websites, period!

# 9) Content Management System & Automation. Content Management System (CMS).

This is the engine of an e-commerce website. It's the back-end administration that has been organized and structured for you the retailer to add products, process orders, handle returns and to display content and products in an organized fashion on the website, for the user to then interactively purchase products.

It is critical to look at the back-end CMS of your proposed website before you hand over any money. Take it for a test drive demo and see if it's easy to use, easy to understand, if it has a clean and organized user interface and a good user manual.

## Flexibility & Speed.

E-commerce Content Management Systems need to be flexible and fast for product amendments and updates. Basic DIY CMS's use a desktop based system where product updates have to be completed on your local desktop PC and then uploaded each and every time, even if you make a small text change. Alternatively and highly recommended are CSV based CMS solutions where product changes are actioned by downloading and uploading a simple CSV that contains your product catalogue. This offers speed and flexibility, and in particular importing many products at the same time can then be a snap!

> **HOT TIP**
>
> *After making changes get into an habit of checking the live website to ensure everything looks correct and is displayed as you intended without errors.*

*A Good, Robust Content Management System (CMS) Will Have the Following features and Functions from an Exhaustive List:*

- Server-based with CSV
- Manage and structure the product layout, with clear category tiers and hierarchy
- Control prices, shipping, and product features
- Manage related products such as cross-sells and up-sells
- Manage stock and synchronize with back-end systems
- Fully automate on-site SEO process in addition to manual editing
- Manage orders and payments and customer information
- Give the user control over site attributes for SEO and layout performance
- Provide individual user accounts

- Automate and communicate order information with customers

- Create and manage information pages such as *'About'* and *'Contact'*

- Produce various reports and statistics such as *'Most Viewed'* and *'Most Purchased'* products

- Store and handle customer information data for marketing and analysis

- Control and produce discount code vouchers, discount code box visibility, banners, offer images

- Blog module for publishing blogs, vital for communication and SEO

- Product features comparison, wish list, marketing features

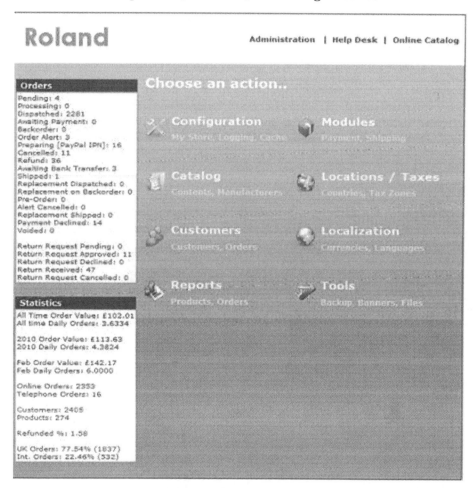

*Simple E-commerce Main Admin Screen - osCommerce Software*

## Automation.

Saves time on many daily tasks that you would otherwise have to complete manually on a daily basis offering flexibility. Many of the e-commerce website owners online are struggling to earn a profit by handling the laborious and mundane tasks themselves. Look to automate wherever possible.

## Synchronization.

Synchronizing processes doubles the effect of automation. This is about linking systems together for the ultimate in efficiency and productivity. Why waste time with manual and duplicated processes?

***Try These to Boost Your Efficiency and Productivity:***

- Set up template emails for every step of the order process—from order receipt to tracking number—so an email is available to send out at the click of a button as and when you change the *'Order Status'* inside of your admin. These emails will personalize and add credibility by extracting and populating the customer's first name automatically from their order data

- Link your products' name fields with your SEO meta page titles, automatically add an H1 Tag to each product name field and add an H2 Tag to your short description field so these 3 are published on the live website without your intervention. Do the same for information pages

- Link your website orders with your back-end accounts system

- Link your stocking system with your live website, giving real-time stock updates

- Where available integrate a Live Data Feed Stock Database from your suppliers into your website

## Order Status Email Templates.

In my back-end e-commerce system, I have 15–20 template emails written and personalized for every e-commerce order status step and covering every eventuality. They simply inform the customer what is happening with their order. When you send them, it updates the status of the order so all back-end users know exactly what the order status is, along with the accompanying notes box.

These emails have immense power in that they reduce customer support enquiries by up to 70% allowing your team to get on with the important tasks. Communication is key!

***Example Template Emails to Reduce Time and Automate:***

- Order Invoice with *'Thanks For Your Order'* message (emailed automatically after a sale)

- Order Shipped or Dispatched

- Product Out of Stock

- Potential Fraud (asking customer to respond within 7 days)

- Customer Loyalty Discount Code (sent automatically after invoice email)

- Product Review Request (sent automatically 10–20 days after order)

- Customer Survey

- Order Refunded

- Trade Account Application, Approval, Decline

***Example Image (below) of Individual Order In E-commerce Back-End Admin Area With Template Emails Linked to Order Status:***

You will see below an individual order. The drop down menu shows the *'Order Status'* template emails, mentioned above. When you select an order status from the drop down list, you can choose to send the template email—attached to each status—to your customer or not. You can also see the order status history in the colored text, so you know exactly where each order is in the shipping process. There is an admin box for internal comments.

The red buttons you see below are linked to dispatch email templates and include shipping details and tracking numbers. When you dispatch an order you click the appropriate shipping company (red button) and enter the customer's tracking number, click *'Send'* and it fires out a template email, confirming the order has been shipped.

***Individual Order Screen from E-commerce Admin (Back-End) - Showing Order Status and History Plus Template Emails On Drop-Down Menu***

# 10) Key E-commerce Features.

E-commerce software solutions are NOT all created equal. Look online, find websites you like, and make a note of features and modules that you want now and in the future. As mentioned before, if you get your full feature and module requirement list in the initial build, you will save money later on. Simply deactivate the features you do not need when you launch.

***E-commerce Feature Ideas from an Exhaustive List of Possible Features:***

- Clean and SEO-friendly design with SEO modules all automated and editable in back-end admin area. Required to gain top rankings effortlessly in the major Search Engine results: Google, Bing & Yahoo.

- Easy to use and sales-oriented design and customer-friendly layout

- Individual customer account log-in area so they can check orders, notes, arrange returns, update personal details, leave product reviews, manage subscriptions

- Simple to navigate admin area to access orders, reports, manage returns, make site changes, set up discount codes

- Manage products: add, amend, hide or remove products, change prices, add discounts, all in a snap and with ease

- Manage Info Pages: add, amend, hide or remove info pages

- Printable order form to fax to suppliers or for transferring to email via clipboard

- Automated post sale e-mail sequence for each status of an order keeping support enquiries to an absolute minimum

- Email order status templates including email tracking number to customer upon dispatch

- Product features including product comparison module

- Marketing features: deal of the week, cross-sells, recommended products, outlet.

- Order confirmation page displays order data (to prevent post-sale enquiries), cross-sells, customer survey and Adsense to make money on the exit click

- Email to customers, print invoices, send out special offers, get newsletter sign-ups

- Multiple discount coupons (% or $/£/Euro/etc.) for customers so you can run deals, special offers, give free shipping

- Comprehensive sales reports of sales per day, week, month, country, product

- Product reports of best selling products, most viewed products

- Exportable statistical reports to CSV format, Doc, Print

- Wish List - So visitors can save products to reference and buy later

- Newsletter opt-in within the checkout with exportable CSV

- Trade area to set up a trade discounts (based on percentage or fixed amount) if you wish to add trade accounts. Each trade customer can have a different discount applied

- Trade 30 Day invoices raised and emailed automatically

- Banner manager to display your hot products or services at the top of each category or other location

- Multiple currencies (Dollar, GBP, Euro, etc.)

- Multiple Languages

- Checkout features - 100% secure, flawless design with detailed step by step instructions to prevent dropped carts

- 1 Page checkout could increase conversions and reduce dropped carts

- Integrated split testing, multivariate testing with reports

# 11) Operations & Order Management.

A busy and successful e-commerce website will handle thousands of orders plus per month, so the management of this is crucial to save time and keep costs down. Everything from payments to shipping and returns needs to be managed easily and effortlessly, so that customers get their orders on time every time, while being updated at every step via your email communication.

Everything is controlled, handled, monitored and processed from the back-end CMS admin area. This is literally the engine room of a website. The best-suited software for you is one that can be synchronized with your existing systems, giving you optimal automation, efficiency and productivity.

***The Main Tasks of Operations:***

- Order stock, pricing, product management

- Take orders online and by phone (if you accept phone orders)

- Handle payments, order amendments and refunds

- Make decisions on suspected fraudulent orders

- Process & ship orders

- Speak with customers about order security issues such as potential fraud

- Speak with customer about any shipping requirements (for example if sending frozen goods you need to ensure the customer is available to sign for delivery)

- Submit claims to your shipping company for any lost orders

121

- Provide customer support and technical support (if required)
- Process returns

### Handling Suspected Fraud.

This is in addition to having the necessary fraud prevention measures in place as suggested in (section 6 Payment), including 3-D Secure, MasterCard SecureCode and Verified by Visa. You can also take the following steps with any orders you feel are potential fraud:

1) Log in to your e-commerce admin and send your template fraud email that you have pre-written. This is located in your Order Status menu. When you send the email, the status of this specific order will then become *'Potential Fraud'* until you get a response. The email itself will detail there is a minor issue with the order and you need the customer to call you to discuss within *'X Days'*

2) If you have no response within your requested timescale then either delete the order or do what we do and call the customer to see if the order and payment are genuine or not. You will intuitively pick up clues from the conversation. Most fraudulent buyers will give incorrect phone numbers, incorrect email addresses, and other incorrect info. Also, fraudsters very rarely answer the phone when you call them. Go with your gut response on these orders

# 12) Information Pages.

These key information pages and how-to guides are important to support your e-commerce product pages, reinforce your terms and conditions, offer trust and ultimately add to the sales potential by providing help and assistance. As discussed in the products section, it is good to give some of this information on the actual product page, as an information resource box or links. The more information your prospect already has, and the fewer distractions, when they are ready to order, the more chance you have of converting their visit into a sale.

These pages can help and assist new visitors entering your website with any concerns or answer questions prior to viewing your product pages. In the checkout area of the website these pages are not required, but small *'info'* links with a small pop up on hover will help with any usability issues.

I like to include the information and technical pages in one area to keep it compact and together, highly focused and easy to access via a *'Help'*, *'Customer Support'* or *'Customer Support'* link.

### Information Pages Could Include:

- About
- Contact

- Shipping (Delivery)
- Security
- Ordering & Payment
- FAQ (Frequently Asked Questions)
- Privacy Policy
- Customer Comments (Testimonials)
- Newsletter Sign-Up
- Technical Guides

**Parking Dynamics Customer Support**

## Site Information

 **Contact Us**
Contact Parking Dynamics

 **How to Order**
Using our website and placing an order

 **Delivery**
Delivery Information

 **Security**
Website & payment security information

 **Ordering & Payment**
How to order & accepted payment methods

 **Guarantees and Returns**
Guarantee and Product Return Information

 **Customer Feedback**
Customer Comments, Testimonials and Feedback

## Technical Information

 **Frequently Asked Questions**
Get Answers to Our Most Frequently Asked Questions

 **Technical Information**
Parking Dynamics PD1 Technical Information

 **Troubleshooting**
PD1 Troubleshooting and Fault Diagnosis

 **Downloads**
FREE Parking Sensor Downloads

 **Installation**
Parking Dynamics PD1 Installation Guides

 **Electromagnetic Parking Sensor Buyers Guide**
Electromagnetic Parking Sensor Buyers Guide

 **About Parking Dynamics**
Information & Company Profile

 **Parking Sensors**
Electromagnetic Parking Sensor vs Ultrasonic Parking Sensor Technology

*Clear & Simple 'Support/Information' Page Layout Example*

**HOT TIP**

*Keep your Information Pages short and simple. Get to the point quickly and give the reader exactly what they are looking for. Use Amazon and other good websites as examples. Most of the pages won't be used for SEO so the use of keywords is not essential. Here is a website of mine (since sold) I wrote all of the info Pages copy for in 2008: http://www.parkingdynamics.co.uk/Support*

# 13) Security, Trust & Testimonials.

Many internet users and especially new users are concerned about disclosing their credit card and personal information to a website and have doubts as to whether you will actually fulfill their order. This can be for a number of reasons, including the media reinforcing this with its reports about ID theft. In addition, they may have personally experienced bad service provided by other websites and offline businesses. Inept service is very common online.

To counteract these concerns and build immediate trust you have to make them feel comfortable and safe on your website. Offer various ways to contact you (phone, email, live chat), display and offer money-back guarantees, trust logos, accreditations and testimonials, and maybe even case studies of happy and satisfied customers.

*Services Available to Build Trust On Your Website:*

- **Trust Logos and Accreditations (US & Global):** BBB.org, Truste.com, McAfeeSecure.com, Comodo.com, Trustedstores.com, MasterCard.com/securecode, Visa.com/verifiedbyvisa, credit card logos, payment service provider or payment gateway and bank logos

- **Trust Logos and Accreditations (UK):** FSB.org.uk, ISIS & IDIS (imrg.org/idis), McAfeeSecure.com, Comodo.com, MasterCard.com/securecode, Visaeurope. com, credit card logos, payment service provider or payment gateway and bank logos

- **Contact:** phone, email, customer support center, live chat, skype, community support software, Facebook, Google+

- **Other Website Features & Logos:** testimonials, case studies, 100% secure checkout (SSL certificate) such as GeoTrust.com, Verisign.com, Money Back Guarantee logos

*Example Trust Logos & Info Boxes to Demonstrate Trust*

## Where to Place Trust Logos & Customer Testimonials:

Placing a few in your left or right hand columns of the website and having a complete testimonial page (see image below) will help reinforce your trust. It will show prospects that other customers have bought from you and have had a great experience. People like to do what other people have done and testimonials and case studies reinforce this behavior. These elements are endorsements and build credibility when utilized well.

**Customers Comments**

Here you'll find a selection of emails sent to us from our 1000's of Happy Customers.

In Car iPod.com is commited to providing the best possible service to our customers and we welcome your comments - either positive or negative. We thank you in advance for any comments/suggestions which you may make. Please click here to contact us.

Hi Gang,

Thanks so much for a smooth transaction and fast Delivery, 24 hours from Order to Installation.

My Dension Gateway product is without doubt the best product I've ever bought for my car. I now have the option to play my iPod, Hard Drive, USB, CD Changer all from the 1 unit. This is one serious gadget!

Thank you and all the best,

**Simon Connor**

A BIG Thanks to InCarIpod.com

Being new to online shopping I'm still a bit tentative about handing over my card details to a website,

*Example of a Full Page Displaying Testimonials In a Uniform Fashion*

125

## Product Reviews.

Having sold a product, then after 10–20 days it's a great idea to email your customers and ask if they would *'be so kind as to leave a product review on the website'.* You can automate this and email them the exact product they have purchased with a link and how-to information, so they can leave a product review easily and effortlessly on the actual product page. This works very well.

The benefit is you will get positive comments about your products, therefore enticing prospects to buy. You will then have product pages that are busy with lots of activity and fresh new content for SEO purposes, as Google loves a site with ever-changing content.

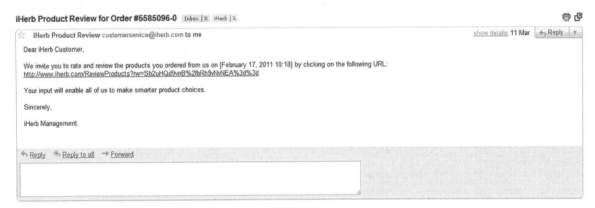

*Example Customer 'Review Request' Email - Automated*

## Review User Interface.

On the next image, you will see that iHerb.com have a simple, yet user-friendly interface for reading and posting reviews. With an interface like this, customers will know where to leave reviews once they get an automated *'leave review'* email—approximately within 10–20 days of receiving their order from you. This is a great layout to employ on your site.

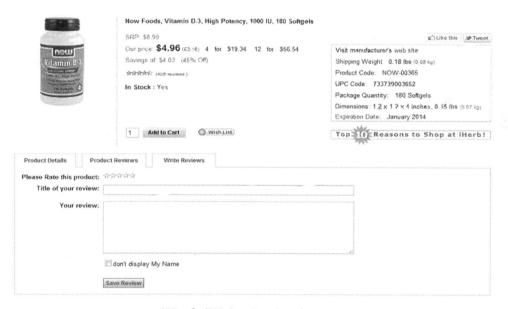

*iherb.com 'Customer Reviews Page' Allowing Prospects to See What Others Have Experienced Using This Product. The Tab to the Right Is Where Customers Write & Submit Reviews. Simple and Clinical User Interface.*

*iHerb 'Write Review' Page*

# 14) Marketing Elements.

To maximize visitor actions on your website—whether they order or not—you first need to get them there. Then you can get visitors to do what you want them to do, be it place an order, sign up for RSS feed, download a free report or opt-in to your newsletter.

It is imperative to build a relationship with prospective and existing customers and that you communicate with them often. Blogs, email newsletters, podcasts, RSS and social bookmarking are five key communication options you have and this includes video blogs known as vlogs. In addition, you can even use RSS delivery for the pro motion of your products such as Best Sellers and New Arrivals. Working in synergy, these give you a superior marketing assault.

## Blogs.

A Blog also known as *'weblog'* is a specific blogging software or module. This is a dedicated area on your website displaying key information for your site users. You can post blog articles there about your business, your website features and services you offer. You can talk about products, new products, special offer products, discount deals, voucher code giveaways, free reports, and promotional videos just about anything. Just keep the blogs around the 300–400 words, don't bore people, get to the point, give lots of value and post them often for full SEO effect.

*On your navigation bar have a button/link called 'Blog', 'News', 'Latest News' or similar.*

There is a feature within your blogging software allowing users to comment on your blog posts. This is something that you can turn on or off based on the desired interactivity that you wish your website to have. If you activate it, just beware of spam and negative comments. UGC (User Generated Content) on the whole is very powerful.

When you have written and published blogs on your live website, there is a *'Ping Option'*—within the back-end of your blog—this will inform the blog directories and blog search engines, such as Technorati.com that a new blog has just been published. This is great for SEO.

I recommend WordPress.com for your blogging software. It has clean code, loads fast, and has a great user interface and lots of SEO goodies. Any good e-commerce developer will have heard of WordPress and used it.

Blogs are very powerful as an SEO strategy and rank extremely fast and very high in the Google search results. You can also synchronize your blog with your email newsletter, so that when a blog is created, newsletter subscribers are emailed alerting them of a new blog post.

- www.wordpress.org (WordPress blogging software)
- www.aweber.com (Email newsletter software - can sync blog and newsletter)

## Email Newsletters.

You can build a highly responsive email list using high quality email software such as Aweber.com or an integrated email module built into your e-commerce software. Generally this will be split into two separate list areas; (1) Front-End Acquisition (before the sale) and (2) Back-End Marketing (after the sale).

1) The first email list is generated from an opt-in subscribe box on your website,

be it in the template of the website (left or right hand column or footer) or on a dedicated newsletter page. You can use basic *'Sign up for our newsletter'* type text or you can push a free report, free how-to guide or specific tips related to your products. Be creative for your specific website and products

2) The second is a list of email addresses extracted from customer order information. Incidentally, when a customer buys from you they legally give you permission to contact them via email with additional, relevant information, products, promotions or special offers. See the CAN-SPAM Act of 2003 for more information

## Where Possible Synchronize the Two Email Lists.

If you can synchronize the front-end and back-end email lists, this will reduce customer frustration. Because once a prospect buys your product and becomes a customer, they will transfer from the front-end list to your back-end email list. The ideal scenario is to automate this process.

It's not always feasible to synchronize two different branded-software lists so your customer may just have to *'Unsubscribe'* from your front-end list instead.

**Note:** When using these two email list models you should legally display—under the CAN Spam Act— an *'Unsubscribe'* link in the footer of emails you send out. If a recipient is not happy about you contacting them, they can simply click the link.

### HOT TIP

*Good email software gives you the opportunity to 'change email addresses' as well as unsubscribe when you click the 'Unsubscribe' link. This feature is critical, as you could lose customers who only want to update their email addresses.*

## Typical User Scenario.

I have all my newsletter subscriptions and order receipts going to different email addresses for better organization. If companies start emailing my invoice account with newsletters it's useless to me as I won't read them – for the ones that offer an *'update email address'* option, I amend it, but for the others I get highly frustrated and just unsubscribe. Be flexible and give both options.

## How Often Should You Email Your Customers?

The best answer I can give is to contact them as often as you can, but always provide information that is valuable to them; advice, tips or with new or special offer products. However, if you bombard your customers too often with product offers, this can do more harm than good and your customers will unsubscribe from your email list.

Amazon manages their email newsletter exceptionally well and offers products related to customers' previous purchases - this is a good example of personalization.

## Email Personalization.

By personalizing the contact you make with your customer, you not only build a relationship and trust, you also increase your sales. This means emailing products based on your customers' historical buying data, laser-focusing your offerings to them. Additionally it is a good idea to use their first name in the emails (Dear Steve, Hi Steve, or Hello Mr Smith), but this depends on your positioning. More below and in Step 4.

*Personalized Email Example, Offering Recommendations Based On Customers' Buying History - Automated for Optimum Efficiency*

*Email Services from the Hundreds of Companies Found Online:*

- Aweber: www.aweber.com
- GetResponse: www.getresponse.com
- iContact: www.icontact.com (Cheapest)

## On-Site Articles.

These are different to the SEO-focused articles posted on article directories. They are of higher quality and are for your on-site visitors in addition to generating SEO traffic. Buyer's guides, product guides, how-to and technical articles all written with persuasion to sell your products while optimized will rank exceptionally well in Google.

Use your imagination here and ask yourself *'what help would I like when buying online'* and mix this in with keyword research mentioned in Step 1, No. 3). because this will not only tell you what information people want, you also build keyword friendly articles at the same time.

Think about your prospects fears, frustrations and problems and answer these in your articles. Go for a solid length of at least 800 words.

## Podcasts.

A podcast is a series of digital media files either audio or video released episodically and downloaded through web syndication. Depending on what products you sell it may be a good way to get people on your email list to subscribe and to communicate with the key benefits weekly or monthly so they eventually buy your products. Podcasts work very well for information services and products in my experience.

## RSS (Real Simple Syndication).

 Is a way of delivering a piece of information from your website to your prospects via an RSS Reader, that displays your content on their PC, Mac, Laptop, Phone, Tablet, Slate or PDA in an easy to view way. An RSS feed could be applied to your blogs posts, blog comments, site content, podcasts, best sellers page, new arrivals page. The concept is that when you add new content this automatically goes to your RSS subscribers' reader, delivering fresh new content in real time. Fast becoming the favored way of staying in touch due to increasing unreliability of email.

## Social Bookmarking.

More and more people regardless of age and income are using Social Bookmarking websites to communicate with one another, via websites such as Twitter, Facebook and Google+. So grab a free bookmark chicklet button from any of the websites online and display it site wide in your site template for easy sharing of your information:

*Social Bookmarking Chicklet Box By 'AddThis.com'*

A user on your website simply clicks the share icon—of the social site they are a member of—to store, tag and share your site page (link) with their *'friends'* or *'followers'.* This gives your site users a great way to stay connected to your company's offerings and to share your products, blogs and information with family, friends, work colleagues and people with similar interests.

## Discount Voucher Codes.

These are also known as coupon codes, retail codes, voucher codes, discount vouchers or even promotional codes. They are number or letter-based codes generated by your e-commerce Discount Code Module in the back-end admin area of your website and pre-determined by you. For example, you could have *'Discount10'* that reduces the order value by a set percentage or a set amount such as or 10% or $10. You can even give free shipping *'FREESHIPPING'* for example.

To apply the discount, your customer will enter this code into a small box during the checkout phase of your website. Then when they click update, the discount will be applied. See the Tip below on why the option to display this box needs to be flexible.

### *You Can Distribute Discount Codes Via:*

- Discount Code websites, Blogs, RSS feeds, videos
- In your newsletter or even as incentive to opt-in to your newsletter
- Social Media including Twitter, Facebook
- Display them visibly on your site or in promotional banners
- In-print marketing
- With all new customer orders (in the box) or in the order receipt email, for a set percentage or set value amount reduced off subsequent orders (Back-End Marketing via email or in the box)
- On the coupon/discount voucher code websites

### *Popular Voucher Code Websites:*

- www.couponcodes4u.com  (US)
- www.myretailcodes.com  (US)
- www.vouchercodes.co.uk  (UK)
- www.myvouchercodes.co.uk  (UK)

## Website Personalization & Recommendations.

In addition to personalizing your email newsletters, you can greatly increase sales by improving your users' experience with product offerings and recommendations. On the front-end (pre-sale) you can add cross-sell modules to your website allowing you to link products together, and incentivize customers to order multiple items per order as opposed to just one. For example, you can link a car stereo with an installation kit or even installation service.

Amazon links products together such as books with books or cross-link products such as CD's with DVD's. Amazon even offers discounts when you buy the two products it recommends, together. The heading for this is *'Frequently Bought Together'*, offered in addition to *'Customers Who Bought This Also Item Bought'*. This means that on the same product page you will see anything up to five cross sell and recommendation marketing blocks and features.

***You Can Call These Blocks or Modules Anything Along the Lines of:***

- You May Also Like, You Might Also Like
- You May Also Be Interested In, You Might Also Be Interested In
- Your Recommendations, Product Recommendations, Service Recommendations
- Customers Also Bought, Customers Who Bought This Item Also Bought
- Frequently Bought Together

**Frequently Bought Together**

Customers buy this album with Heligoland ~ Massive Attack

 +

**Price For Both: $22.98**

[ Add both to Cart ]  [ Add both to Wish List ]

One of these items ships sooner than the other. Show details

***1 of 2 Examples of Amazon's On-Site Recommendation Boxes***

Heligoland ~ Massive
Attack
$9.99

Emotional Technology ~
BT
★★★★☆ (359)
$15.98

Ima ~ BT
★★★★★ (38)
$19.98

For Lack of a Better
Name ~ Deadmau5
★★★★★ (11)
$13.99

*2 of 2 Examples of Amazon's On-Site Recommendation Boxes*

And on the back-end, after your prospect has ordered and is now a customer, using the same principle you can offer them personalized recommendations using *'Recommendation Engines & Systems'.*

## Recommendation Systems.

When a returning customer is logged into their account on your website, then by analyzing and using their historical buying data, you can promote and recommend specific products they should buy. These can be related products, associated products, and accessory products pertaining to their original purchase and preferences. Use your creativity to offer more products. *See Amazon.com for ideas and read more in Back-end Marketing (Step 4).*

### *Areas of the Website That Can Be Personalized with Recommendations:*

- *'Related Products'* block, *'You May Also Like'* block, *'You May Also Be Interested In'* block

- *'Frequently Bought Together'* block

- Home Page

- Products Pages

- Order Confirmation page

- Best Sellers or Top Selling Products

- New Products or New Arrivals

- Emails

- Wish List

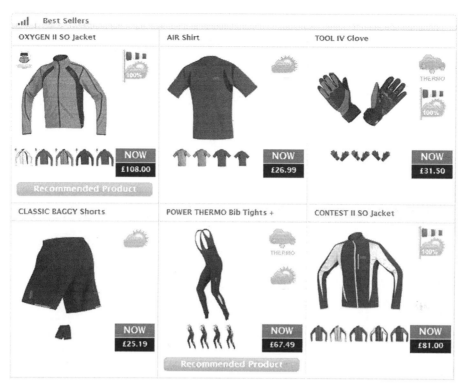

*Example 'Best Sellers' Page That Extracts & Displays Best Selling Products from Actual Sales Data In the E-commerce Back-End for Optimum Automation & Synchronization*

## Adsense.

I mention Google Adsense in my recommended Google Tools, because it's an easy way to make money on site exits. For example, out of every one hundred visitors to your site on average 99% will leave without taking your desired action. So having Adsense gives you the opportunity to make money when people exit your site.

You can position your Adsense block within your products or main site template and give it a title such as: *'Customers Also Liked'* or *'You May Also Be Interested In'*, which helps it integrate into your site. Alternatively, you could position it as *'Site Sponsors'* or just have it showing as Google ads. Adsense is also ideal for putting on the Order Confirmation page or even Contact or Newsletter Opt-in Confirmation pages.

*2 Examples Using Google's Adsense Boxes to Make Money On the 'Exit Click'*

- Google Adsense: www.google.com/adsense

# 15) Analytics, Reports & Measuring.

Analyzing website user data and analytics is critical if you want to stay ahead of your product category and market, beat your competitors in the search engines, and build and target your website specifically for your users. When you analyze the data on offer on a daily, weekly or monthly basis, it gives you an up-to-the-moment, bird's eye view of what is really happening on your website and online.

The first time you look at your website stats you will be very surprised and will learn some important and key lessons. As a result of analyzing and using this data, you can consistently refine your website to higher profits by:

- Targeting top keywords and key phrases

- Selling products people actually want

- Targeting specific products to specific customers

- Making usability changes to your website, content, products and checkout to boost sales literally overnight

- Setting goals and responding to the results

- Hiding products that do not sell, but are good traffic generators, in a corner of your website

### Do You Know Your Bounce Rate?

Bounce Rate is a measurement that expresses the percentage of site visitors that enter a single page on your website, and leave without clicking to another page. This is measured in Google Analytics. Bounce rates are reduced by making your website more 'sticky' as detailed in 'Design'.

### Do You Know Who Your Visitors are?

This is key information if you are only selling to one country. When you look at your statistics, you will find that the majority of your site visitors come from other countries. You may be losing 80% of your traffic because they cannot buy from you!

Are your users Windows, Linux or Apple Mac users? What is their screen resolution? When does your traffic peak in a 24 hour, weekly, monthly or annual cycle? All of these questions and more will be answered by analyzing site data.

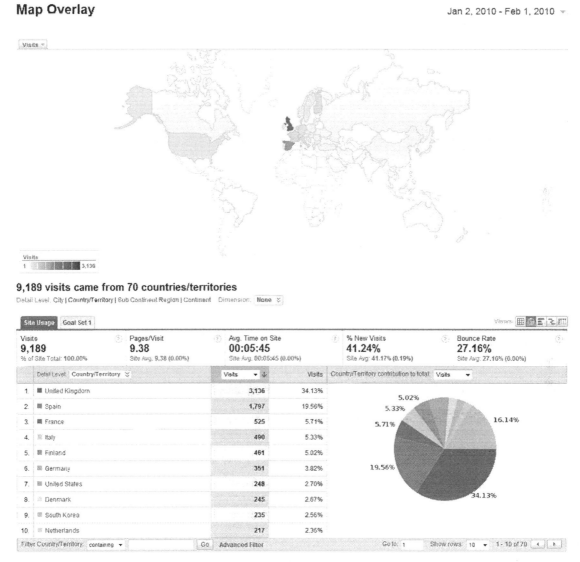

*One of the Many Google Analytics Reports Showing Various Website User Data*

## You Need Traffic To Analyze.

It's important you get your website traffic up to a reasonable number before you start to analyze, respond and refine your site. If you start with only 10 visitors a day this is not enough to measure and act upon. You need a good mixture of visitors from different demographics and I would wait until you get at least 50–100 people a day so you have enough metrics to judge and get actual and reliable results. The more visitors per day the more accurate the data will be.

I also recommend analyzing at least 90 days to 180 days (3 months to 6 months) at a time, as this will give you a very good mix of users and a good time scale to look at users' habits and behaviors.

***Three Ways to Get User Data:***

1. Add Google Analytics code to your website... it's really easy.

   Google Analytics is comprehensive and will tell you everything you need to know about your site user's habits: the buttons and links they click and those they ignore; how much traffic you get and from what country; bounce rates; where they abandon your checkout process; plus lots more information. Your web developer should know about Google analytics – if not, turn and run!

   - Sign up for Google Analytics here: www.google.com/analytics

2. With all standard hosting accounts, you get Web Stats (known as server logs) found in your CPanel (Control Panel). You will need to ask your host for the username and password to access these. Common server stats are AWStats and Webalizer.

3. Your e-commerce software will come with its own reports, statistics and data too. Great for analyzing orders, sales, refunds and product related information.

## Test. Test. Test.

Testing and refining is about taking your e-commerce website and business to continually higher levels of growth using the principles detailed in the Key site Elements such as Design, Usability and Conversion. If you analyze, you can respond positively to your available data, reports and statistics—on a monthly basis as a minimum with weekly or daily being optimum. Your competitors will not know what has hit them. The more testing you do and the more website refinement you can implement, ultimately the more products you will sell!

Successful websites including Amazon often run multiple tests on their website daily to gather data and respond to the results. They test everything from a simple image placement on their homepage, product layout, Add to Cart buttons, images, text, colors through to the messages and products you see when you have placed an order— the order confirmation page.

## Key Data to Measure.

Here is a brief overview of the key metrics of your website to measure so you can refine your traffic source and quality, lower your bounce rate and increase your conversion rate.

- **Unique Visitors or Absolute Unique Visitors** – How many individual people came to your site in a day, week, month or year. This is a key statistic to determine if your traffic is consistently growing, remaining static or declining each day, week or month. Do not use visits or hits - use unique visits as this shows you each unique person as one visit.

## Determining Your Visitor-to-Sales Ratio (Conversion Rate):

For example: (a) 1000 unique visitors per day enter your website and (b) 10 individual orders are placed within this period. You divide the number of unique visits by the total number of orders to determine the visitor-to-sales ratio.

**Conversion Rate Calculation:** (a) 1000 divide by (b) 10 = Conversion Rate (i.e. 1 person in every 100 visitors orders from your website)

**Expressed As a Percentage:** (b) 10 divide by (a) 1000 x 100 = Conversion Rate of 1%

To determine your monthly or annual visitor-to-sales ratio use the same calculation but add up your total unique visits and orders placed within your desired period of time.

**Note:** Do not use total number of items sold as some people buy more than 1 item per order. You can filter this data further by splitting visits by specific country of origin.

- **Page Views** – Page views is the total number of pages viewed on your site and is a general measure of how much your site is used. It is more useful as a basic indicator of the traffic load on your site and server rather than as a marketing measure.

- **Bounce Rate** – Bounce Rate is the percentage of single-page visits (i.e. visits in which the person entered and left your site on the same page without clicking to another page in your site). Bounce Rate is a measure of visit and traffic quality and a high Bounce Rate typically indicates that site entrance (landing) pages aren't relevant to your visitors. You can minimize Bounce Rates by tailoring landing pages to each keyword and ad that you run. Landing pages should provide the information and services that were promised in the ad copy (the advertising that drew the visitor to your site in the first place).

- **Time On Site** – Time on Site is one way of measuring visit quality. If visitors spend a long time visiting your site, they may be interacting extensively with it. However, Time on Site can be misleading because visitors often leave browser windows open when they are not actually viewing or using your site.

- **New vs. Returning Visits** – A high number of new visitors suggests that you are successful at driving traffic to your site while a high number of return visitors suggests that the site content is engaging enough for visitors to come back. You can see how frequently visitors return and how many times they return.

- **Country of Origin of Visitor (Map Overlay)** – Determine what country and territory your visitors are coming from. Use the available data maps to visualize volume (visits, page views) and quality (page views per visit, conversion rates, per visit value) metrics by geographic region.

**Note:** It's important to determine your Visitor-to-Sales Conversion Rate by country as it may be better than you at first thought. If 30% of your traffic is from overseas but you only ship nationally then you can discard the international Unique Visits data from this calculation.

- **Direct Traffic** – Establish who clicked a bookmark to come to your site or typed your site URL into their browser and find out how they compare to the *'average'* visitor to your site. Direct traffic can include visitors recruited via offline (i.e. print, television) campaigns. You can also segment direct visits by city, visitor type, or other factors.

- **Search Engine Traffic** – How much search engine traffic do you get and how does this compare to traffic as a whole to your website? Find out which search engine your traffic comes from. The available graphs detail overall trends from the various search engine traffic.

- **Keywords** – Establish what keywords and key phrases your visitors are using to find your website. Available graphs show overall trends from each keyword and its traffic origin. You can segment the traffic referrals from each keyword by city, visitor type, or other factors.

## What Are Conversion Goals?

Goal conversions are the primary metric for measuring how well your site fulfills specific objectives. A goal is a website page a visitor reaches once they have made a purchase or completed another desired action, such as completing a contact form, registration or download.

## How Can Goals Help Me?

Once you have set your goals, you'll be able to see conversion rates and the monetary value of the traffic you receive. You can also define a *'funnel path'* for each goal. A funnel path is the path you want visitors to take to reach a goal. Defining a funnel path allows you to monitor how frequently visitors who begin a conversion process actually complete it.

- **Goal 1 (Checkout Cart Abandonment)** – Set up this goal funnel on your checkout process from Shopping Cart (Basket) page through each page and step to your Order Confirmation Page. This will clearly breakdown and detail how many people enter and leave at each step and how many people complete the checkout process and order from you.

- **Goal 2 (Contact Form Submission)** – Use this goal to determine how many people enter your contact form page and how many people actually submit the form to you. Great for seeing if your contact form actually works.

**Best Viewed Products**

| No. | Products | Viewed |
|---|---|---|
| 01. | PHANTOM II JACKET (English) | 8370 |
| 02. | ALP X II Jacket - sale (English) | 5213 |
| 03. | COSMO WS JACKET (English) | 3722 |
| 04. | POWER III Bib Tights short - Spring & Summer (English) | 2875 |
| 05. | OXYGEN III JACKET (English) | 2851 |
| 06. | OXYGEN II SO Jacket (English) | 2788 |
| 07. | GT II SOCKS (English) | 2633 |
| 08. | Mistral III Glove - sale (English) | 2589 |
| 09. | FUSION II Jacket - Sale (English) | 2070 |
| 10. | ALP X ZIP-OFF JACKET (English) | 1971 |
| 11. | COUNTDOWN III JACKET (English) | 1960 |
| 12. | GORE SEALED DERAILLEUR CABLES (STD) (English) | 1914 |
| 13. | CONTEST II SO Jacket (English) | 1858 |
| 14. | XENON RACE JACKET (English) | 1822 |
| 15. | OZON AS JERSEY (English) | 1793 |
| 16. | TOOL III Jacket (English) | 1787 |
| 17. | XENON THERMO Bib Tights + (English) | 1746 |
| 18. | ALP X II Jacket (English) | 1641 |
| 19. | GLOVES VULCANO LADY - sale (English) | 1632 |
| 20. | MTB SPORT BIKE SOCKS (English) | 1622 |

Displaying 1 to 20 (of **485** products)          << Page 1 ▼ of 25 >>

*'Most Products Viewed' Report Taken from osCommerce Back-End Admin*

**Best Products Purchased**

| No. | Products | Purchased |
|---|---|---|
| 01. | PHANTOM II JACKET | 95 |
| 02. | GORE SEALED DERAILLEUR CABLES (STD) | 47 |
| 03. | ALP X II Jacket - sale | 43 |
| 04. | POWER III Bib Tights short - Spring & Summer | 41 |
| 05. | XENON SO Glove | 34 |
| 06. | Custom Product #1 | 33 |
| 07. | FACEWARMER III | 31 |
| 08. | OXYGEN II SO Jacket | 28 |
| 09. | AIR Shirt | 27 |
| 10. | GT II SOCKS | 27 |
| 11. | OXYGEN SO Bib Tights + | 25 |
| 12. | OZON AS JERSEY | 25 |
| 13. | HELMET IV Cap | 24 |
| 14. | ZOOM Shirt - sale | 24 |
| 15. | BIONIC II Shirt | 22 |
| 16. | XENON II JERSEY (LEAVE OFF LINE UNTIL Feb 2010) | 22 |
| 17. | COSMO WS JACKET | 19 |
| 18. | ALP X SOCKS PACK OF 1 | 18 |
| 19. | ALP X ZIP-OFF JACKET | 18 |
| 20. | COUNTDOWN VEST | 18 |

Displaying 1 to 20 (of **364** products)          << Page 1 ▼ of 19 >>

*'Most Products Purchased' Report Taken from osCommerce Back-End Admin*

**Sales Report**

Start Date:
1 ▼ February ▼ 2010 ▼
End Date:
2 ▼ March ▼ 2010 ▼

[Show]

☐ Pending  ☐ PROCESSING  ☐ Dispatched  ☐ Awaiting Payment (PayPal)  ☐ Refund
☐ European Warehouse Processing  ☐ Telephone Order  ☐ Customer Returns  ☐ BACKORDER  ☐ Order Alert
☐ ORDER UPDATE  ☐ Cancelled  ☐ AWAITING CUSTOMER RESPONSE  ☐ Replacement Shipped  ☐ BANK QUERIES
☐ IN STOCK - DISPATCHING  ☐ In-Stock

| Date | Order Number | Customer Name | Price (ex) | VAT | Total (inc) | Shipping Cost | Total + Shipping |
|---|---|---|---|---|---|---|---|
| 01/02/2010 | 602183 | | £68.94 | £0.00 | £68.94 | £8.95 | £77.89 |
| 01/02/2010 | 602184 | | £180.00 | £0.00 | £180.00 | £15.95 | £195.95 |
| 01/02/2010 | 602185 | | £84.26 | £14.74 | £99.00 | £0.00 | £99.00 |
| 01/02/2010 | 602186 | | £149.34 | £26.13 | £175.47 | £0.00 | £175.47 |
| 01/02/2010 | 602187 | | £26.81 | £4.69 | £31.50 | £6.00 | £37.50 |
| 01/02/2010 | 602188 | | £59.57 | £10.42 | £69.99 | £6.00 | £75.99 |
| 6 Orders: 01/02/2010 - 01/02/2010 | | Totals | £568.92 | £55.98 | £624.90 | £36.90 | £661.80 |

*'Sales Report' Taken from osCommerce Back-End Admin*

141

# Website Launch Essentials

When launching your website ensure your web developer sets up and installs these prior to launch. This will ensure your website is optimized for Google, reporting and for testing.

## 1. Google Account or Google Apps Account.

Google Account and Google Apps both offer similar services and one of these will keep all your Google tools and reports in the one account. For example you could use Gmail which is Google's server based email service for your email client if you prefer that to a locally PC based email client.

The benefit of Google Apps, is it allows you to have multiple email aliases (sales@, info@, etc.) for the one domain and gives you the option to use your actual domain in your email such as info@yoursite.com whereas the basic Google Accounts using Gmail does not give you these two features. See the full list of recommended Google Apps under *'Tools & Resources'* at the end of the book.

- Google Accounts: www.google.com/accounts
- Google Apps: www.google.com/apps

## 2. Google Webmaster Tools.

Google Webmaster Tools gives you some great features to maximize and promote your website with Google. Get your webmaster to add an **XML sitemap** so whenever you amend or add a page to your website Google knows instantly.

**Preferred Domain:** Allows you to inform Google which URL (domain name) you prefer and want it to index in its search index. Its recommended to submit using the full URL: http://www.your-site.com as opposed to http://yoursite.com. Most people will link to your main URL, be it organically (natural linking) or by request. If you have both URLs in Google's index then your incoming link quantity (Link Popularity) will be split between the two URLs, weakening the SEO power of each one.

**Canonicalization:** rel="canonical" - This attribute gives you control over how your URL's appear in the search results. Ideal for product pages that may be accessed through different URL's such as www.yoursite.com/blue-shirt or http://www.yoursite.com/products?category=shirts&color=blue&cruel=no. This helps to reduce Duplicate Content.

**Sitelinks** is a key feature of Google Webmaster Tools. These links are shown below the site URL in only *'some'* Google search results. They are typically only awarded to leading sites per market. The links essentially give searchers a shortcut to popular pages within a given website and these links can be changed within Webmaster Tools. So select and link to important pages on your site via these sitelinks.

142

- View Google Webmaster Tools: www.google.com/webmasters/tools

## 3. Site Submission.

### In Addition to Setting Up Webmaster Tools I Also Like to Either...

a) Manually submit my sites to Google's index at the below web address, or...

b) Link to my new website from an existing website that Google's spiders (robots) visit on a daily or regular basis. This is the quickest way to get your website indexed in Google, via an already live site.

### Submit Your New Website to Google's Index When Its Launched:

- www.google.com/addurl (US and Global)

- www.google.co.uk/addurl (UK )

Now that your website is in development it is time to get ready to launch. Before you do, it is important to run some quick tests to check for leaks in the system. Better you find them than your customers...

# Five Pre-Launch Testing Requisites

## 1) Cross Browser & Platform Testing.

Test your website for load speed, correct operation, and usability, ensuring all design and layout elements are in alignment on the page and in the correct locations. Also, test the screen resolution to ensure the site table fits as intended in your users' browsers without a scroll bar appearing at the bottom. If your web designer has built the site correctly it will auto adjust for different screen resolutions.

I recommend you actually run these tests in addition to your web developer, as you will often spot things off balance that they miss.

Open your website in all browsers on (PC, Laptop, Mobile Phone, Tablet and Apple Mac) with different operating systems and browser versions including but not limited to Internet Explorer (Versions 6, 7, 8 & 9), Firefox (versions 2, 3, 4 & 5), Google Chrome, Opera and Safari. If you can't get all of these specific browsers and platforms to test, then check with your friends, family and work colleagues. More often than not they will have older versions of the operating systems and browsers.

## 2) W3C & Google Compliant.

Tim Berners-Lee is the director of the W3C (World Wide Web Consortium). Since 1994 the W3C has provided the guidelines by which websites and web pages should be structured and created. The rules they outline are based on best practices. While websites don't have to comply to be viewed correctly in Internet Explorer and other popular browsers, there are a number of compelling reasons why you or your designer should ensure that the W3C guidelines are followed and that your site is brought into compliance.

Having said all that, don't get too hung up on errors the W3C validation tool throws up, as it's pretty pedantic. Putting it another way - if your site looks good in all browsers when you test, what else do you really need? You can run a check in the link below:

- W3C Validator: http://validator.w3.org

### Google Compliant.

As Google is currently the number one search engine where most of a site's organic traffic will come from, I focus on making my website's Google compliant as opposed to W3C compliant. Follow the Google Webmaster Guidelines and Google's Help Notes and you'll be good to go.

- Google Webmaster Guidelines: www.google.com/support/webmasters

**Google Website Translator.**

If you are using the Google Language Translator module, check for the positioning of text headers and formatting site-wide (across the entire website). As different languages result in words having more letters, this could push one line onto the next line break.

**Note:** Any text overflow present, when your default language is converted, is something you may just have to accept. So weigh up the *'cost'* of this text overflow versus the simplicity of using this module, and the extra sales you could get as a result of selling globally.

## 3) Checkout Test.

Test the entire order process or *'sales funnel'* from site entry to order confirmation page. Is it easy to navigate to products? To select quantity, size, color—or other options (attributes)? Does your cart page work correctly and is it clear for customers what they should do next?

Actually complete the order yourself, in order to test. Go through the checkout page or pages and read the text. Does it read well and fluently making you understand the next step and then the next step in this process? Look at the buttons. Are they positioned correctly and are they the right size and color? Does the wording on your buttons make you want to click them?

When you get into the checkout area, is your SSL security certificate working? Are you getting the visible padlock symbol in your browser and has the web address (URL) changed to *'https'* as opposed to http?

Is it easy to enter your card details? Is it seamless between you and your payment gateway system—depending on type of payment set up and integration method used—on your website or off your website if you process offline? Does your payment gateway-process your orders fast or is there a long delay and does it hang for 30 to 60 seconds?

If so you will lose customers, so iron this resistance out. Do error messages appear when you place test transactions? Do the error messages make sense and provide the appropriate action steps for your would-be-customer to continue with their order successfully?

When you have ordered, are you getting the order confirmation page? Does everything work on here? Are emails including the order receipt email, dispatch email, backorder email, product review email, all working and does the order status feature in your back-end admin work? Ensure you check all of this because your web designer will not!

## 4) Website Forms & Email.

Test all forms and form confirmation pages. Test any contact forms and your email to ensure you have pre-sales and after-sales contact. If you are using support center software, test this in all areas for correct operation and communication to your back-end systems. The same goes for any other forms you may have, including email newsletter opt-in forms... give them all a thorough workout.

How many times have you submitted a contact form on a website and not been presented with a contact confirmation page with a confirmation message? Just some simple reassurance like *"Thanks for Emailing Us, We have received your contact message and will endeavour to respond within the hour"*. And when you didn't get this page and/or message response, I know 100% you were left scratching your head wondering if the website you'd just emailed had received your enquiry or not.

So use this page to give a confirmation message and links back to the home page or some other area of your website you deem important. You could even place your email newsletter form on this page with an inviting opt-in message and/or place Google Adsense on here to make money on the exit click.

Without this working efficiently customers will just get frustrated!

## 5) Usability Test.

Or as I like to call it, the *'Mom Test'* (that's *'Mum'* if you're in the UK). Having made site changes including website usability, text, image and button changes, I like to test these on my parents, friends and family or anyone who I know who is inexperienced online.

Many websites can learn from this simple philosophy. How many sites have you been on—obviously designed by techies with large foreheads—that just don't make logical sense and make you say out loud, *"what are they thinking"*?

And don't worry - this is not some cruel or lame experiment! Essentially, what I am saying is that after making site changes, it's good to take a step back and ask someone not involved with your website—especially inexperienced web users—to see if they can comfortably use your website effectively without resistance.

This will quickly find any problem areas in your design and usability. Remember, you have to build an e-commerce site for all ages, personality types, intelligence levels and for people with all degrees of internet experience.

### It's Now Time to Build Your Feature-Rich E-commerce Website...

If you have chosen the route of using branded e-commerce software through an established site design and development company, the next step is preparing a brief so your potential site builders can review and respond with a quotation.

This should be clear and concise yet with sufficient information to cover all aspects of the build and the features and modules you require. The quotes should follow your brief where possible so you can compare with quotes from other companies.

*In Step 3 We're Going to Look At How You Can Find an Exceptional Web Designer or Development Team So You Can Launch Your Website and Hit the Ground Running...*

# Step 3—
# Get Hiring

## How to Find a Kick-Ass Web Designer!

→ **Discover Top Tips for Hiring a Kick-Ass Web Designer!**

→ **Why the 'Typical' Hiring a Web Designer Approach Is Bad!**

→ **Find Out If Your Web Designers Are Working for Your Profit or Theirs!**

→ **How to Communicate Your Web Brief for Optimum Design!**

→ **10 Things Your Web Designer Doesn't Want You to Know!**

→ **How to Avoid Getting Outsource-Slapped!**

→ **Why Using a Contract Could Protect You & Your Ideas!**

→ **Eliminate Years of Stress, Headaches & Problems!**

# Why Most Website Owners Get Disillusioned...
# and Their Websites Eventually Fail!

Why is it 97% of e-commerce websites struggle to make profits for their first 3 years after launch, and most eventually crash and burn? Well - it all starts with your design team. Working with the right team can mean the difference between success, or imminent and painful failure!

*Note: In this chapter the term 'web designers' covers web developers, web agencies, freelancers.*

### 'Hiring a Web Designer' – A Typical E-commerce Website Buying Experience.

I've dealt with many e-commerce designers and developers since 2000 and have spoken with many e-commerce site owners and project managers since then. Let me share with you a mindset and pattern that has become apparent, and that essentially creates the unnecessary struggle leading to failure and ultimately bankruptcy.

*You Will See In Steps 2 & 3 Below How Critically Important Finding a Good Web Designer Is:*

---

1) Customer approaches web design company with brief for a quotation...

2) Web designer promises exceptional site design and Top 10 SEO rankings...

3) Website is built, customer pays in full and the website is handed over. However no training or insights into e-commerce business success are given!

**At this point a new website owner has no idea about Traffic > Conversion > Relationships!**

4) After 3 months of low or no sales, customer thinks they need a big fat budget to spend on SEO and marketing to make money online...

5) Customer gets disillusioned with limited sales, increasing costs and no profits...

6) Customer blames *'the internet'* for simply not being a way to make money...

7) Year 1–5: customer quits and closes the website down, with a big pile of personal or business debt!

---

# Web Agency Warning:

Finding a web agency that has sold online themselves is pretty rare. If you do find one, it typically goes something like this... *The owner has sold a bit online, usually on eBay, who then hires a designer that has sold a bit online, usually on eBay, who works with an SEO that has sold a bit online, more often than not on eBay.*

Although eBay and dedicated e-commerce websites are both e-commerce, they are 2 very different animals and require different models and skill-sets. Not many people who have sold online themselves through a dedicated e-commerce store and have experienced real SUCCESS, actually tell others how to do it. It's rare.

Web Agencies, especially large web agencies have a team of people who all work together including: sales, developers, designers, usability and technical support. Each person from each department *'knows a bit'* and they then attempt to sync all of this knowledge together through a project manager who handles multiple projects at any one time.

### Why Is It Important to Find an E-commerce Developer That Has Sold Online Themselves and Not Just On eBay?

### 1. Lack of Experience

How can someone without the actual year-on-year experience of the full e-commerce lifecycle *'Source, Stock, Sell, Ship, Support'* help a small-to-medium size business sell online? Like most e-commerce companies their employees come straight from university where most of their experience is learned from a university text book or from corporate backgrounds where budgets are massive.

### 2. Poor Focus and Input On Your Project

Add to the lack of experience, how much time is your project manger likely to give to you when they are running multiple projects at the same time?

### 3. The University & Corporate Approach

Its true! Most web agencies are run by post-graduate students that have learned their knowledge at university, or corporates that have learned only a small area of ecommerce. Compare real world *been-there-done-it* experience vs. learning from a tutor and a text book. Think about this seriously if you want Real Results!

### 4. Corporate Costs = Astronomical Prices

Web agencies typcially work with big corporate companies that have huge web budgets and they both speak the same BS corporate language.

Very few agencies have the backbone and experience of being *in-the-trenches* with an e-commerce business, who have earned the e-commerce stripes to then help you from Start-Up to Cash Exit and everything else in between.

*So, let's start with a simple 'e-commerce quotation' to help you select the right e-commerce company to build your web store...*

152

# Effectively Communicating Your Website Brief to a Web Designer

Effective and regular communication with your design team is essential to ensure you start on the right path, execute quickly and efficiently, and produce an e-commerce website that ultimately sells products in big numbers and makes a great profit.

## Getting a Quotation.

For a detailed and accurate quotation, based on your exact specification and requirements, your designer will commonly email you a *'project brief form'* to complete and return. This covers most aspects of the website build including logo, design, feature list and modules required.

The quality and detail of this form will differ from designer to designer. If you need to send additional details, do so as and when you think of them. However, to help the designer and keep communication simple do your best to get it all in 1–3 emails.

Before you complete the *'project brief form'* I recommend drawing an outline of the website design as you visualize it on paper, or on your PC using MindMaps (Mindjet MindManager), Word, Visio or Evernote. List the site structure and layout as you see it, together with the feature list and modules required. I personally find it useful to grab a pen and paper and let my creativity flow through a brain dump. I later transfer this onto the PC in an organized structure and into easy-to-understand words for the designer, sent in an email with visual attachments.

## Let Your Designer's Creativity Flow.

When completing the design aspect of the brief you can be as detailed, or as vague as you wish but give your designer some creative freedom. What I mean by this is, when you find a good designer be careful you do not give too much information that may get in the way of the designer's creative skills. I like to give them the site concept, layout, and features required and let them to do the initial mock design selecting colors, images and copy alignment. I then refine where required to finalize the design.

***Site Build Specifics to Email to Potential Designer:***

- Detail your goals for the website such as: Concept, Target Customer and Positioning. Essentially, what is the site about, what will it give you and what will it get you?
- Get a delivery date for the mock and live site and list the pre-launch protocol
- Email 5 websites you like the design of and detail why

- Detail the design concept (layout, site structure, logo, fonts, and maybe colors, basic text location.)

- List the features and modules you will need (number of products, product variables, order and admin features, returns, SEO, marketing, reports)

- How many sales you expect, what revenue you want daily, monthly, annually?

- Add as many points of your own, as you see fit

# How to Hire a High Quality Web Designer

You now have a solid e-commerce foundation, mindset and philosophy, and you know exactly what features, modules and options you want in your website. It's now time to hire a Website Designer using the below top tips.

An exceptional web designer, developer or team will have great communication and fully understand your e-commerce goals based on experience. They will then produce a website that works towards your goals, not just to bolster their own portfolio.

## Are They Working for Your Benefit?

Unfortunately for you, the majority of web agencies couldn't care less if you succeed or fail and just see each project as a wage. They turn over project after project to keep the sales momentum, so the bills are covered. Very few companies will ever contact you to see how your business is doing with regards your sales and profits, and if you have successfully implemented traffic, conversions and back-end marketing.

It is actually in their best interests to see how they can improve these three key areas for you. Some website performance changes could lead to a stronger portfolio for them. This is just another example of the lack of awareness of marketing on the back-end, for them.

## Individual Designers vs. Design Team.

There are some great individual web designers available for hire who work for themselves, but a big word of warning; there are only so many hours in a day and these tend to work Monday to Friday.

You need to establish, how much time they can allocate to your project with regards initial build and after sales support and updates. I am not saying big design teams are better, as you may get more focused attention from one-on-one designers.

***Here Are Some Points to Consider:***

- Who can provide the most time and attention for your initial build and updates?
- Do they have the experience as individual or collectively as a team?
- If you are dealing with a web agency, can you speak directly with the designer or do you have to go through a project manager? Relaying information through a project manager can cause miscommunication and frustration
- If you have marketing deadlines to meet and need site changes such as promo-

tional banners or graphics, will your designer do whatever it takes to meet your schedule?

- If you spot errors on the website or if the *'code breaks'* (it happens, especially after updates), when will it be fixed? A design team may provide 24/7 support, an individual simply cannot

- Does your web designer or team pick up the phone if you call? Many will only communicate by email. Email, Phone and Instant Messenger such as Skype?

- If your website hosting fails at 9pm and your site goes down, is someone available to fix it?

- Does your web team have seamless communication between the different departments to implement your ideas correctly and on time

- Do they have a newsletter or method of alerting you to new features & modules they develop, which is critical to further developing your website and business?

# Ten Tips for Finding and Interviewing a Kick-Ass Web Designer

### 1) Are They Working for Your Benefit?

Is this a value-for-value exchange? Is the design company or individual working for your benefit, are they taking a deep interest in your business and its success, or are they just concerned about their bottom line? Many companies hand over your website, take your cash and swiftly disappear. You need to know they have an interest in the results you get and are there to support you and help to develop your website as trends and technology evolves.

Do their current clients' e-commerce websites actually make a profit? Can they give you some success examples and specific numbers? Not many can, as most e-commerce sites bomb!

Is a system in place for alerting and updating you to new developments, for example if they develop new features and site modules that will benefit your website and business? It is critical you stay on the e-commerce cutting-edge.

### 2) Do They Understand Your Website and Design Goals?

Does your design team fully understand your goals? Select a web designer who understands e-commerce business in addition to great design. Ensure they have an e-commerce portfolio with a design style you like and an available demo site so you can take a test drive.

What is the point in buying a website that does not work? You would not drive a new car out of the dealership with a flat tire. So get a website exactly as you want it, and one that works!

Can and will they make appropriate recommendations with regards the features and modules required for your business? This is crucial for automation, synchronization, efficiency and productivity.

### 3) Communication and Support.

Communication is essential before, during and after the project. Is communication limited to email or do they take calls or instant messenger such as Skype? What are their working hours and will they bend to accommodate important deadlines for you? E-commerce websites are a 24/7/365 business model - don't forget that!

Ensure they can provide support manuals and videos for the e-commerce software back-end admin and provide after sales training and support. I can guarantee you will need it, until you are comfortable and experienced with the software.

What if the site code breaks and you spot errors, how fast can they fix it and do you have to pay for these corrections?

### 4) Designer Availability.

When you have found a website design you like, establish if the original designer is available and will be working on your project. Many companies especially those on the outsource websites such as Elance, have a quick turnover of staff so this is important to find out.

Also find out do they outsource themselves? This is critical, as many companies simply take your order and pass the project on to another agency or designer. This is not a problem if the Project Manager handling your project is exceptional, but very few PM's are of this quality in my experience. This could lead to delays, support issues in the future and big frustration for you in the long term.

### 5) Get Protected.

Where possible get them to sign a contract that explicitly specifies four things.

1) The project or service they are providing you (for example Web Design)

2) The delivery time for the project to be completed (for example 3 weeks)

3) The total cost for the project (for example $1500)

4) All intellectual property rights that make up the website are 100% yours and they cannot use or replicate, this work again, unless they first consult with you and pay you an agreed amount. You can also agree to share or you give them permission to use your development work again if you wish. I've paid big sums of money for the time to build bespoke modules, only for my designer to use this on other sites at no cost. Big mistake!

*Read More About This Contract At: www.ecommercegetitright.com/get-protected*

## Top Questions to Ask:

### 6) Detailed Quotation.

Get your designer to detail all of the costs and completion delivery times for the website build in a written quotation, be it by email or letter. Get them to specifically detail:

- Cost and delivery time for the initial mock design? (mock should be free)

- Do you get unlimited revisions on the mock until you are happy with the design?

- Cost and delivery time for the initial website build? (typically a one off price)

- Cost for updates (typically billed per hour)?

- Cost for support?

- Cost for code error corrections?

- Cost for SEO management and is this optional? (you will typically get better results at a lower cost with a specialist SEO company)

- Cost for hosting if they are hosting your website?

- Can you deactivate features and modules you do not need to use at launch, but want to activate later, and what is the cost for activation later?

**Note:** You could even set penalties for late delivery times where possible and within reason, such as getting a 10% discount. Show them you are a serious business owner and won't accept inferior service.

### 7) *Domain Name Ownership.*

Ask - *"Can I register my own domain name, giving me full ownership and control and can I then point the Name Servers to your server?"* (if they actually host your website). Taking control of your own domain name will prevent any problems over ownership in the future and will give you full control if you wish to move designers or servers later on.

### 8) *100% Intellectual Property Rights?*

When they have built your website, will they hand over all the intellectual property rights to you? This means: are you the 100% legal owner of the whole website, including e-commerce CMS software, design, logo, graphics, images, text and web content?

### 9) *Design Skills.*

Ask, *"What software do you use to design?"* If they hard code with HTML they will usually have more skills and produce a better site with more features and more flexibility than someone who uses Adobe Dreamweaver or another WYSIWYG (What you See Is What You Get) software such as Microsoft Expression Web or XsitePro.

### 10) *Are They Experts?*

Do they have an outstanding portfolio and the knowledge to back it up? Ask them to explain, how they will structure your website for customer usability and conversion and for SEO purposes—for the search engine spiders. Ask them directly *"what is your model or formula for design specifics like alignment, colors and font?"* If they cannot answer these Q's with great articulation and passion, then find a new designer.

# Additional Points:

## a) Mock Design.

Ensure your designer uploads your mock design onto a live test site (URL), so you can see exactly what it will look like on a live site. View as 100% size in a live browser with full design implemented as intended. Many designers are lazy and will send you a 50% completed mock design as a jpg image. Viewing as a mock image often gives a poor reflection of the intended quality and site design, especially if you cannot view as 100% size, this happens in some picture viewers. Also, get them to design the mock in various color schemes so you can select your favorite. This is very easy for them to do and gives you more options.

If they give you an incomplete mock, get them to complete it first before making a decision. An incomplete mock is like seeing an architect's plan for your new house that shows only the floor area, and no side elevation, no windows, no doors, no roof, no stairs. It's hard to visualize the finished product, and impossible to assess its suitability.

## b) Hosting.

If they provide you with hosting, ensure their servers are of the highest quality, have as close to 100% uptime as possible, can provide you with secure hosting via SSL and that you fully understand their hosting charges, be it monthly or annually. What is the support provided if the site goes down?

# Ten Things Your Web Designer May Not Want You to Know!

As we now know, web agencies, designers, developers and graphic designers are not all created equal or even as good as they claim to be. Do they cover things up? If so, what do they commonly hide?

**1) You Must Register and Be the Sole Controller of Your Domain Name... And Retain 100% Intellectual Property Rights to Your Website.**

Always buy and register your own domain name and forward the name servers to the server and hosting company where your website is hosted. If your design company insists that they wish to buy and control the domain, turn and run!

There are a massive number of people and businesses that have been slapped by web companies unwilling to play fair. They will not release the ownership and control over to the rightful owner. This tends to happen when the customer realizes they want full control of the domain, so they can move to a new designer.

On a website I built for a client, it took about 6 months of negotiations and frustration to (a) locate the company in control of the name, (b) get a transfer deal sorted and (c) get them to actually action the transfer.

A big tip is to make sure you register your domain name before revealing it to anyone, as some bandits will go and register it quick, as soon as you mention it and try to charge you a fortune for it!

Your website intellectual property rights also need protection. Make sure from the outset you have 100% legal ownership of software, images, text, logos created for your site. If they want to use any aspect of your site, which you conceived and built, such as bespoke modules and features, then they have to pay you for it at your desired asking price. Where possible, get them to sign a contract to back-up this agreement.

## 2) Who Is Designing Your Website?

When you highlight a website design as one you like, before agreeing to hire a designer it is essential to establish who built the website you like. Then find out if the original designer is available to build your website. Every person on the planet has his or her own perception of a clean, dynamic and professional website. So whatever your website brief, you need a designer who has the same perspective as you do, based on existing site designs you have seen.

### 3) What Level of Service Do They Provide to Support You and Your Website... 24/7/365?

Most web companies have no idea and no interest in your business or your long-term success, fact! They like to build you a website, take your money, add the site to their portfolio and disappear. But they are very interested if you are happy to spend more on a monthly maintenance fee or for *'SEO'*—as some companies position it. Be very wary of these services unless you get a detailed plan of what they are doing and what you are getting for your money. Results are all that counts, so offer to pay on results, and see if you're dealing with professionals or just hot air!

Do your best to find a company or developer who has the X Factor! Hire someone that has an interest in your business results and growth and communicates well. If they provide you with hosting find out what they will charge, and what their uptime is (you'll need uptime very close to 100%.)

It's also critical to establish what handover training they will give you and your team when your site goes live. Is it a 30 minute demo of the back-end and then they say goodbye? Is it just *'ring or email with any questions at any time?'* Do they charge for this? If you are new to e-commerce, you will without a doubt need help getting familiar with the software and processes.

### 4) Running a Profitable E-commerce Website Is Not Easy.

*Do you recall the **Traffic > Conversion > Relationship** model?*

Miss this foundational strategy and fail to implement this and the other tips in this book – and competitors will absolutely take the sales you miss. You need to work hard to attract customers and convince them to buy from you, and that's only part of it. You also have to buy products, handle products, ship products, deal with customer service and all the other elements of an e-commerce business. There is a lot of work involved without a doubt. It comes down to how much you want it to be successful.

You have heard the superlatives that are essential to achieve success like creativity, passion and tenacity. While these are good traits to have, it's also vital to build on a solid foundation of planning, common sense and watching the financials and the numbers.

You will never achieve a successful e-commerce business, or any business for that matter, working on recreational time. You need to put in the hours, and even if you outsource the majority of tasks, you still need to keep in touch and watch your outsourcer team, marketing, sales and profits to stay on target.

### 5) Your Competitors Are Constantly Trying to Get Ahead of You In the Search Engine Rankings.

Business is business and if you do not take the sales on offer, a competitor will gladly take them from you. So watch them closely, monitor their websites often, and use

Google Alerts and software such as Copernic Tracker. If you follow the strategies in this book and on www.IanDaniel.com you will have the robust foundations you need to kick ass in e-commerce and SEO!

## 6) If You Do Not Update Your Website Often, You Will Lose Business.

Follow the principles in the book by blogging at least once every 1 to 3 days where time and money allows. If you can, add keyword rich blogs daily and allow blog comments so site users post new and regular content, but watch for spam and negativity. Also, continue to add keyword rich articles and how-to guides often. Add a customer review module so your product pages get *fresh content* as and when a new product review is submitted—and frequently with your product keyword or key phrase in the review. Also add new products, where feasible, on an ongoing basis.

This does not mean change your home page, info page or product page content every week, just to make *'changes'*. It means keep updating and adding site pages in a way that brings value to your customers and gets you further along to your business goals. Ultimately do not let your site stagnate.

## 7) Customers Will Not Find Your Website Just Because It Is Live.

Unfortunately Yes! As we discussed in the *'97% of e-commerce sites make $0 profits in their first 3 years'* statistic, this means you should be marketing your website on a weekly basis, if not daily. Spend time working on your website as opposed to working in your business running it. However, this is the big challenge especially when it comes to e-commerce, which is why using efficient systems, automation, and speed are essential.

There is an old quote about business *'early to bed, early to rise, work like hell and advertise'.* The point here is the word *'advertise'.* Without it your business will never reach its full potential. You have to be assertive and not passive; I would even upgrade assertive to aggressive!

## 8) You Need to Test Your Website Across Multiple Browsers and Platforms.

It's very important to check your website daily by simply skipping through the key pages, categories and processes to ensure all is working fine. Websites and HTML can break without warning especially after updates (for example, if your web developer uploads and downloads product CSVs often.) If people cannot view your site in their chosen browser or platform, your sales will be hit.

Open your website in all browsers (on a PC, Laptop, Mobile, Tablet and Apple Mac) including but not limited to Internet Explorer (Versions 6, 7, 8, 9), Firefox (versions 2, 3,4, 5), Google Chrome, Opera and Safari. If you cannot get all of these specific browsers to test, ask your friends, family and work colleagues. More often than not they will have older versions of these browsers and operating systems.

Also incoprate a *'Report Problem'* or *'Feedback'* form on your website, visible on all pages so helpful site users will report a bug if they find one.

### 9) Your Website Should Be Built Using CSS and a CMS to Work Faster and More Efficiently.

Ensure your developers build your website using CSS (Cascading Style Sheets) so the html code is clean, which essentially means it will load fast, Google can easily index your site and if you make changes to design elements, these can be replicated across the site in a snap, as opposed to updating every page independently. Also, build your e-commerce site using a Content Management System (CMS) software. This is the engine of your website: it's a high quality, robust back-end software allowing easy customer and product management, products additions, order processing and returns.

### 10) You Could Save Money Into the Future If You Get All of Your Required Features In the Initial Website Build.

You will need to quiz your developers on this, but in my experience if you do not get as much of your future start-up site development work, features and modules as you believe you will need into your initial site build, you will have unnecessary costs later on. This is because the initial build is generally charged at a set price, and updates will be billed by the hourly rate (normally $50 plus per hour.)

Therefore, brain dump what you want from the site now and into the future. Modules and features you do not need when you launch can simply be deactivated until you need them and switched on later.

# My Story: Hiring Inept Web Designers & Crooks

My internet experience began in Feb 2000, 2 months prior to the Dot Bomb era when the big *'investment hungry'* internet businesses imploded, changing the value of web businesses forever. At the time, I sold and installed car audio products such as CD players, speakers, amps, etc., to local offline customers. The business was only 6 months old at this point when I discovered the internet through a media frenzy in my local area.

The local news on TV visited an internet company who sold domains, hosting and websites. They themselves were only about 6 months old but were raking in money left and right from unsuspecting, and very internet naive customers, who had no suspicion in April 2000 that 5-page websites they were currently paying thousands for would suddenly be worth about 80% less. This was the dot.com crash, when investors suddenly realized the value of web businesses had been massively over inflated!

I say *'frenzy'* above. In the office of this web company was an electronic scoreboard and an alarm. Every time a sales rep sold a website over the phone, the bell would ring and the scoreboard would add another *'sale'* on. Not only that, but the office members would jump to their feet and party every time the alarm rang! However, this was not destined to last for long, and the company no longer exists...

This buzz got me hooked, and I subsequently bought my first domain name and 5–page website called caraudioworx.com from this very company, and it cost me $1000 approx (£1500). It was a brochure website with about three paragraphs of text and one or two images per page. Any good web designer could knock it up now in about an hour. So I had acquired an exciting new revenue stream to add to my existing business model, what could possibly go wrong? Well as it happens, everything pretty much did!

In May 2000 I started to study internet marketing whenever I wasn't driving my van around the Northwest of England, fitting and selling car audio products. Around this time I bought an accounts software product to handle my books and inside was a free book called '*10 Powerful Marketing Strategies That Make $Millions*' by Paul F. Gorman. This was to change my career and business from that day.

I wanted to learn more and became a marketing sponge and subsequently got my hands on Paul Gorman's classic '*How to Out-Sell, Out-Market, Out-Promote, Out-Advertise Everyone Else You Compete Against*'. From this one book I started to write copy and market in the big glossy car magazines, at a big cost. From June to December 2000 I spent $7.5K on advertising, sending traffic directly to my new, killer website.

6 Months later... not a single email, phone call or sale through the site! I was devastated. My credit cards were now maxed out and I was $10K in debt from my first website venture. This included initial purchase, hosting, magazine advertising, banners, flyers and business cards. So much for my new found web skills. January 2001 I shut my first website down!

3 months later I tried again and paid $2000 to a *'back street'* web designer for an e-commerce website this was supposed to have all the e-commerce bells and whistles and 500 products. June 2001 arrived and still no website or web store, so I junked this project too after trying to locate my web designer who had disappeared with my hard-earned cash. I was now $12K in the red on websites and marketing in just 12 months.

### From 2000-2004, Web Designers and E-commerce Software Were Mediocre At Best! But This Cash Problem Had to Change, and Fast...

October 2001, my website *'failure experience'* started to pay off and by Xmas CarAudioPlus.co.uk was turning over good money and from there the very successful InCar-Network.com was born. Incidentally I sold this network early 2007, so please do not contact the current owners.

> ### *'If You Have Any E-commerce Questions, Ask Me At: www.IanDaniel.com'*

I will not bore you with all my other successful and non-successful web investments and *'money squandering'* but I can reveal one thing. Of the 100 plus outsourcers and web companies and individuals I have used, I would only use about 5–10% again. This in itself shows you the overall standard of skill online. Just look on Elance.com and the other outsource websites: not many providers have top feedback ratings.

There is one outsourcing project I would like to mention, to help save you the time, hassle and money I was conned out of. Back in 2003 I was building a feeder site network of 3 information websites to send highly targeted traffic to my then (growing rapidly) car audio and in car-entertainment e-commerce website network, InCar-Network.com.

I posted a project on Elance.com for a *'High Quality Copywriter'*. From the 30 or so responses I got, was a very articulate and polite guy called **Chimezirim** who claimed at the time he was an American based writer. In retrospect I should have Googled him to check.

Anyway as it turned out, this guy was a con artist from Nigeria and because my websites were growing so fast and the business needed my focus, I wasn't giving this project the attention it deserved. I was continually giving the OK for my accountant to transfer money over to him on request and I wasn't checking his work. The result is that I ended up spending about £2K ($3.3K) with nothing in return, as one day he decided to change the passwords to the feeder sites and essentially stole my websites, disappeared and I never heard from him again.

### So What Lessons Have I learned, That Will Help You When Hiring?

- ✓ Avoid pretentious fancy-pants web design agencies and absolutely avoid back street web designers who build websites on the cheap, and can disappear without trace at any time. Check portfolios, testimonials and references from happy customers, and get training and guarantees.

- ✓ Always keep control of your websites. Host them on your server account where possible. If your outsourcer then decides to change your password, you can always get it back from the hosting company because the account is in your name.

- ✓ Ensure good communication on your terms is available. Email, Phone and Skype or other Instant Messenger service for immediate help.

- ✓ If you are running outsource projects, set timelines and delivery dates and check them off as the project is delivered. Keep this plan so you know your targets. Where possible, pay only on results (POR).

- ✓ Do not pay up front. If they need a deposit, then pay a small token deposit and pay in stages as and when the project is delivered. For example, pay a 10% deposit, 40% half way through the build and then the remaining 50% upon completion. Handle the project on your terms and not theirs but make it fair for both parties in case you wish to pull out at any stage.

- ✓ Accept that with most web designers, there is no loyalty. If a bigger and better project comes their way, they won't hesitate in putting your project on hold while they go where the money is.

- ✓ Do your best to protect your work, which you have creatively designed and paid for. Its 100% yours and not the designers. They have merely implemented your ideas and you have paid for that: you legally own the intellectual property rights to this design or software.

- ✓ Do not trust anyone! Be very wary of 'Yes' men who are really nice but very vague and say 'Yes' to everything you ask them. Show them you are the boss and they will respect you in return. **And, don't be afraid to walk away if you not happy with them.**

- You can find out more at: www.IanDaniel.com

*Now Your Website Is In Development or Live, In Step 4 We're Going to Learn How to GET MORE SALES... This Is Internet Marketing for Your E-commerce Website and Business On Steroids!*

# Step 4—
# Get More Sales

## Marketing to Hordes of Hungry, Ready-to-Buy E-commerce Customers!

→ Learn Bullet Proof Front-End (Acquisition) & Back-End Marketing Tactics!

→ Lead Generation, Landing Pages & Conversion Refinement!

→ Explosive SEO (Search Engine Optimization) Strategies!

→ Article Marketing, Blogs, Social & Video!

→ Exclusive E-commerce Marketing Tips & Techniques!

→ Link Building for Rapid Search Rankings!

→ Article Marketing for Quality Content & Traffic!

→ Using an Army of Affiliates to Work On Your Behalf!

→ Blog, RSS, Social & Video Marketing!

→ Back-End Marketing to Increase Sales Up to 35%!

# Marketing Plan

Step 4 is an overview of the marketing strategies available for your e-commerce store. E-commerce marketing does not have to be complex; it is about detailing your plan, forecasting what extra sales you want, setting budgets and measuring your results. If it works and generates sales, keeping doing it and if costs rise but sales do not, try something else.

Having said that, do you need a 20-page marketing plan to get started? No. Simply establish where you are and where you want to be with regards traffic and sales, plan your numbers in a spreadsheet, detail your marketing model in MindManager, Visio, Evernote or Word and take action. Just one thing - it isn't easy finding impartial marketing advice online. I'll do my best in following pages.

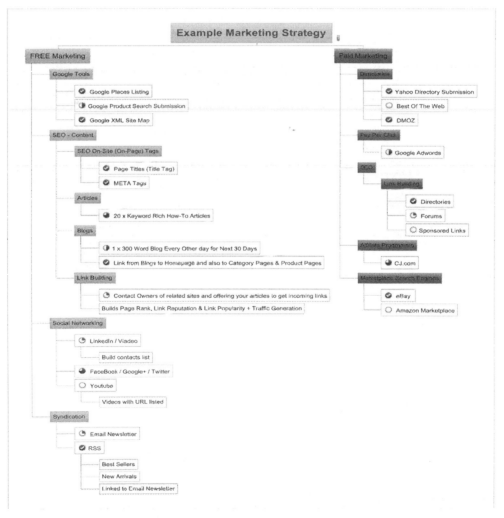

*Simple Example 'FREE vs. Paid' Marketing Strategy Using MindManager*

# Front-End (Acquisition) Marketing

This simply means the process of acquiring new customers to buy your products. After you've invested money on your website build, you then need to attract prospects to your site via marketing. Once they have purchased from you and become your *'customer'* you then use back-end marketing to build a relationship and offer them more products.

## Google Product Search.

Google Product Search (formerly known as Froogle), is a price comparison service launched by Google in 2002. It helps online shoppers find and buy products across the web. As a seller, you can submit your products to Google Product Search, giving your site exposure and allowing shoppers to easily and effortlessly find your products.

### Increase Traffic and Sales.

Product Search connects your products to the shoppers searching for them, helping you drive traffic to your store resulting in sales. Your products will appear on Google Product Search and may even be displayed in the Google search engine results, depending on your items' relevance.

### Submit Products for Free.

Inclusion of your products in Google Product Search is completely free. There are no charges for uploading your items or the additional traffic you receive to your site.

### Reach Qualified Shoppers.

Reach shoppers precisely when they are searching for items to buy on Google.

Google Product Search interface provides a basic search box into which a shopper can type product queries to return lists of vendors selling a particular product, as well as pricing information. Product Search is only available for selected countries.

- Find out more at: www.google.com/products or www.google.co.uk/products

Google Product Search is different from other price comparison services in that it neither charges a listing fee, nor accepts payment for products to show up first. In addition, it makes no commission on sales.

Any company can submit individual and bulk products via two methods:

## Data Feed.

Google recommends creating a data feed which contains all of your content in a single tab-delimited text or XML file. You can send them your data feed directly through your Google Merchant Center account, or by using File Transfer Protocol (FTP). This will make sense to your web designer.

## API.

The Google Base API is designed for developers with technical know-how who would like to integrate their applications with Google Merchant Center. Your application can upload new data, update or delete existing items, and query Google Merchant Center data to find matches for complex attribute criteria. Again, ask your web designer.

*Sign Up for This and More Google E-commerce Tools At the Google Merchant Center:*

- Google Merchant Center: www.google.com/merchants

# The Power of SEO (Search Engine Optimization)!

When your prospect searches for your product in the Google search engine, it conducts a series of simultaneous calculations requiring only a fraction of a second. The results are determined by votes (links to your site, also known as backlinks) and Google's PageRank algorithm, named after Google's co-founder Larry Page. There are over a hundred site elements that Google ranks sites based on, but these 2 are key.

When e-commerce websites are built correctly from the ground up, integrating specific and advanced on-site '*White Hat*' SEO techniques, they become explosive SEO machines! I love and utilize e-commerce combined with SEO techniques for this very reason. White Hat simply means ethical, and in-line with Google's recommended practices.

Successful SEO is built on a formula that once learned can be used on any website and in any market to compete with or even obliterate the big boys.

Halfords.com for example have over four hundred stores in the UK, a massive website and a budget many times bigger than mine, yet they could not compete in the search engines for many competitive terms in the car audio, in-car entertainment market when I competed with them. For example, they could not touch us for terms like '*iPod Car Kit*' and we dominated this competitive online space. They may have had the budget, but unless you know what to do with it, it's pretty useless.

Microsoft **Dynamics**
microsoft.com/uk/everyonegetsit      Build closer customer relations and reach new levels of profitability.

No Holes Parking Sensor | **Parking Dynamics** Reverse Sensor
**Parking Dynamics** - Take the RISK out of Parking and Reversing with the PD1 Car Parking
Sensor - No Holes "invisible when fitted" Front and Rear Car Parking ...
www.**parkingdynamics**.co.uk/ - Cached - Similar

Installation                   Volkswagen
Buy Now                        BMW
Audi                           Fiat
Mercedes Benz                  Chrysler

More results from parkingdynamics.co.uk »

Fitting Reverse **Parking** Sensors | **Parking** Sensor Fitting
Click here for **parking** sensor fitting instructions and our national **parking** sensor fitted
service, with **parking** sensor fitters across the UK.
www.**parkingdynamics**.co.uk/Installation - Cached - Similar

Electromagnetic **Parking** Sensors | No Holes Electromagnetic Sensor
Introducing No Holes in Bumper **Parking Dynamics** PD1 Electromagnetic Parking Sensors...
A Totally Unique and Revolutionary Front & Rear Electromagnetic ...
www.**parkingdynamics**.com/ - Cached - Similar

About **Parking Dynamics** Electromagnetic Parking Sensors
**Parking Dynamics** is the online store of the **Parking Dynamics** PD1 Front and Rear Parking
Sensor and is based in the UK. You can buy online 24/7/365 and we ...
www.**parkingdynamics**.com/about - Cached - Similar

*Top 4 Position Google Ranking With Google Site Links Below the Listing.*
*'Sitelinks' Are Awarded to Category Dominating Websites*
*and Here They List Your Popular Website Page Links*

The SEO foundation and formula for Google, Bing and Yahoo, the big 3 search engines, is pretty much the same and your website should use this formula.

# On-Site (On-Page) SEO Basics:

## 1) Keywords & Key phrases

Lots of high quality keyword and key phrase-rich and fresh content, updated often via articles, blogs, products and customer reviews. Google frowns upon duplicate or plagiarized (stolen) content and the original content always scores the highest in the search results. If you do steal content then you could be dumped out of the search engines, so be warned.

## 2) Meta Tags

Strong on Page Meta Tags: Page Title (Title tag), Description, Keywords and H1, H2 tags. Use of Alt text on images.

## 3) Design

Strategic site design, layout, and structure and site templates that follow the 3 F formula - Fast, Functional and Familiar. Clean code and use of CSS is a must.

## 4) Google Robot Friendly

Implement an easy to follow path for the search engine robots (spiders), ensuring the center container loads first with text and then the header, footer and sides of the main site template. You must use more content in the center container than the other areas of the site template, ensuring each page is unique.

## 5) Optimize PageRank

PageRank Optimization using key strategies, including the *'No Follow'* attribute (see image below). This passes Google PageRank around your site structure to key pages and blocks non-key pages from using up this valuable Google juice.

## 6) Internal Linking

Use key internal linking strategies to pass PageRank around your site as above, but also to gain multiple listings in the Google search results and create your own on-site link machine. Multiple listings equal more search engine real estate—that in turn results in a dominance of your market and more clicks to your website.

## 7) Related Terms

The use of related terms within your content is critical as this gives you an edge. For example if you are selling a HD TV, you would also use terms like Television, DVD, Blu-ray, HDMI, Accessories, Cable, LED, LCD, Surround Sound. These related terms all add to the Google attraction, as it deems your site relevant and you an expert.

## 8) Clean URL's

Use clean URL's such as www.yoursite.com/sony and www.yoursite.com/tv-accessories or www.yoursite.com/sony-tv-accessories

## 9) Create Many pages

The more pages your site has, the more internal links it will have, and consequently it will accumulate and preserve PageRank better. Do not delete pages of products you no longer need. Either 301 redirect these to their replacement pages, or hide them deep within your website and place a keyword rich link to your new page, sending traffic across via a *'This Product has been replaced - Click Here for the New Version'* type of image with an accompanying text link for passing Google goodness.

## 10) Unique Page Titles (Title Tag) & URL's

Every page on your website must have unique page titles and URLS (page names).

> *'Word of Warning! Do Not Rely On Google and Natural Search for 100% of Your Traffic. If Google Ever Changes Its Algorithm and This Is Your Only Traffic Source, Your Business Could Sink!'*

## No Follow Attribute.

Simplified, the No Follow Attribute: **rel="nofollow"** is used within the code of your website. You place it inside of your <a> </a> tags which are links. When used it prevents Google from passing PageRank to the recipient page and used if you don't want that page to rank such as Contact, Privacy, Help, About, How To Order, Security. An advanced SEO strategy but easy to implement.

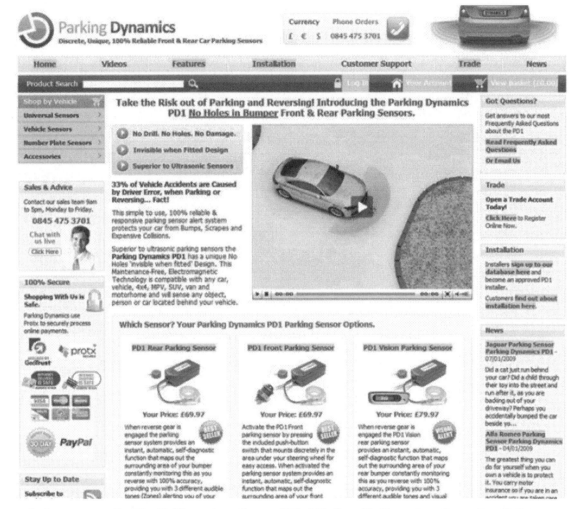

*Website Using the No Follow Attribute (Highlighted) Showing PageRank Distribution. Viewed In FireFox Browser With the 'Quirk Search Status' Add-On*

# Off-Site (Off-Page) SEO Basics.

## Links.

Links to your website are counted by the search engines as votes. Ultimately, the more one-way incoming links (backlinks) you have pointing to your site and key pages in addition to a minimum level of quality per link, the higher your pages and site will rank in the search engine results. However, this formula only works if the on-site (on-page) SEO is rock solid too. Think you can have one without the other and dominate your market? Forget it. You need a strong mix of good on-site and good off-site SEO.

## Organic Link Building.

Once a website launches, if people like the content, products or design and if it is interesting and newsworthy, then it becomes talked about, quickly gaining in popularity, and the brand ultimately gets exposure. What happens next affects your Google Top 10 assault. People who have websites or use websites such as blogs, forums, community and social sites start to talk about you. From this, links are naturally built: the more exposure you get, the more natural and FREE links people will make to your site. This is a big bonus of organic link building!

This can create Massive Momentum! You have heard about the snowball rolling down a hill getting bigger and bigger. This is the same, and the effect is viral! When building a website it is a good idea to choose a domain name with your main keyword and then brand it, so when people naturally link to your site, for example '*TVDirect.com*', they will generally use keywords such as '*TV Direct*' or '*Buy TV*' in the anchor text (the text link pointing to the website). This further bolsters your link reputation.

In line with the points above, if you can highlight something that is news or buzzworthy about your website and products then you can get this powerful viral effect going. It can spread like a virus - Fast!

## Link Bait.

Following on from the above points, give a good reason for other sites to link to yours. Post unique, interesting and useful articles, blogs, videos and information. Run offers, discount codes and promotions. Offer exclusive products and how-to videos and think of ideas to get a buzz going.

## Deep Links.

Links should not only link exclusively to your homepage. Point links to your main category and key product pages too, via external (off-site) or internal (on-site) sources. These are Deep Links. Remember Google ranks pages not websites, so each page is ranked on its own merits, which means each page needs links and PageRank.

## Link Sources.

Here is a list of the many resources you can use for gaining links to your website:

- Blog Commenting
- Forum Commenting
- Article Directories

- Press Releases
- Social Bookmarking
- Social Networking
- Article Distribution
- Shopping Directories
- Affiliate Marketing
- Paid Links

### Main Key Phrases vs. Long Tail Key Phrases.

When you start to perform keyword research, you will find your main key phrases—lots of search volume—will account for approximately 20% of your keywords total, and the 80% of key phrases will have much smaller search volume—these are known as Long Tail key phrases. This means if you target the Long Tail key phrases (the lesser searched for keywords and key phrases) you can get more traffic overall, as added up they swamp the main keywords. This is an essential strategy if you are in a very competitive market, where all the players are targeting the main key phrases. Blogs and articles are ideal for long tail keywords.

Not only that, long tail keywords and phrases rank faster than main keywords and phrases. I've had long tail terms rank top 10 in Google within 1-3 weeks.

- **Main Keyword Example:** Panasonic TV
- **Long Tail Keyword Example:** Panasonic TX-L37V10B LCD TV with Stand

# Google Places.

Formerly known as Google Local, this gives you the opportunity to target your website specifically at local customers. If you optimize your Google Places advert well, you will within time get top ranking positions for your local search main key phrases. In the search result listing itself, you have the benefit of a map, the address of your location, opening times, plus more which greatly emphasizes your listing in the search results.

- Sign up to Google Places for free here: www.google.com/local/add

# Article Marketing.

Content makes the Internet what it is. One of the best marketing and SEO strategies that you can do for your e-commerce site is to write articles—or hire a freelance author to write articles for you—and submit them to the popular article directories. More articles submitted equal more incoming links and more entry pages to your website. This will ultimately provide natural and unique content, which Google loves, and it will also find a keyword rich link back to your website in the article '*resource box*'—found at the bottom of the article.

The fundamental tips for writing and submitting good articles are to keep them around the 400–600 words mark, use a keyword-rich title, use good keywords in the body copy and utilize the resource box and point a text link back to your site by using good keyword-rich, and compelling text. Article marketing is not complex!

*Just a Few from the Hundreds of Article Directories You Can Use to Generate Links Back to Your Website for Your Chosen keywords:*

- www.EzineArticles.com
- www.Amazines.com
- www.ArticleBliss.com
- www.EzineMark.com
- www.ArticleCity.com
- www.ArticleDashboard.com
- www.iSnare.com
- www.GoArticles.com
- www.Upublish.info

- www.vretoolbar.com/articles/directories.php (Top 50 Articles by PageRank)

Plus, there are many more! This is your opportunity to submit unique and product relevant content based on your niche market to a number of article directories. Not only will this establish you as an expert in your industry, but it will also provide a swarm of natural backlinks and traffic to your website.

# Pay Per Click (PPC).

Pay Per Click advertising is a great way to get your website instant traffic by using Google's advertising model (Google Adwords). Microsoft and Yahoo also offer the PPC advertising model but their user interfaces are complex and their search engines cannot get close to Google with regards quantity and quality of users and searchers. I recommend starting with Google and investing your time, energy and money here.

Google Adwords delivers targeted advertising like no other medium. Long gone are the days of wishing and hoping your advertising works. By running tailor-made adverts (Adwords), you are using Google's actual search data, which has been collected and collated every second of every day from millions of searches. It doesn't get more targeted than this.

Essentially Pay Per Click is like an auction. By targeting specific keywords and key phrases, you can get immediate exposure based on your allotted daily budget—you determine this inside of your Adwords account. As an advertiser, you pay Google for every click a visitor makes, when they enter your website through your Adwords advert. It is important to start with small click prices, hone your skills in your particular market or niche and then roll out more adverts once your Click-to-Conversion rate is profitable.

The good news is Google uses two factors *'Relevancy'* and *'Quality Score'* to reward the best Adwords adverts and positions them higher on the page, even if you pay less per click than your rivals. Components making up the Quality Score include your account CTR (Click-Through Rate), the quality of your landing page (i.e. website pages) and relevancy, plus other factors.

When searchers type in a specific search term, the Adwords adverts appear in two sections of the page; at the top and to the right of the natural search engine results. They also appear on *'Product Search'* results and on other private websites as *'Adsense'*. They will also list on *'matching content'* sites via the Adwords Contextual Advertising option within your Adwords account. I recommend you switch off the Contextual Advertising Option as it is relatively inefficient at matching ads with relevant websites, in my experience that is.

The use of Adwords banner ads is an open market right now with low click fees and lots of opportunity without the high competition. Success with Adwords takes time, means creating lots of ads and testing and refining as you develop your skill set. This means creating many Adwords accounts, each with its own Campaigns, Ad Groups and keywords. But again, start small and grow as your skill-set grows.

To create multiple Adwords accounts and to keep them all in one place use Adwords Client Center. And make sure you let Google know that you are an *'Advertiser'* when creating this one big account by selecting this option in the set-up. To easily manage your big list of keywords try Adwords Editor.

- Create a Google Adwords Account: www.adwords.google.com
- Adwords Client Center: www.google.com/adwords/MyClientCenter
- Adwords Editor: www.google.com/adwordseditor

# Landing Pages.

A landing page can be any page on your website or off your website you specifically send traffic too with the aim of converting into a sale. By *'off your website'*, I mean specific pages built off-site or not linked to your other site pages as part of the normal site structure.

Landing pages (also known as squeeze pages) are used as a powerful lead generation tactic, and optimizing these via split testing and multivariate testing can super-charge your profits. The idea behind landing pages is to decrease bounce rate and on the flip side to increase visitor response and stickiness on your website. Bounce rate, if you recall, is determined by the number of visitors that enter on a specific page on your website and leave on the same page without clicking to another page. As already discussed less than one in every one hundred visitors to your website will convert (buy, opt-in to your newsletter, contact you, complete a survey) and the rest will leave without taking action or doing your most wanted response.

Landing pages are designed to send potential customers (prospects) directly to individual, bespoke and tailor made pages—via Google Adwords or other sources—before they are shown your main product website. This is to build a relationship prior to offering information and products to them. E-commerce websites very rarely use landing pages but they can be very powerful when used correctly. Further to your advantage is the fact that not many people even know how to build them effectively, especially for e-commerce websites. However, if you try to run landing pages as part of your marketing strategy and get it wrong, you could lose even more customers before they even see your main product site.

You can use landing pages to capture email opt-ins or get a sale by taking visitors directly to a specific product. Landing pages are often used to capture the prospect's name and email address in exchange for an incentive such as a free report, how-to guide or a discount code for your e-commerce store. You can then use this new lead to contact via email marketing to promote your e-commerce site and products.

You need to weigh up your bounce rate and visitor-to-sales conversion rate and optimize these as well as you can, prior to implementing landing pages. When new customers enter your website, are they finding the info and products they need and are they converting? Or do you first need to communicate with them and build a relationship via your email list, by giving a free report, free video or other technique using the landing page tactic?

**Note:** Using PPC with landing pages will laser-focus your marketing and attract only your target customer. This should improve conversions when done right.

# Split Testing and Multivariate Testing.

Most e-commerce websites do not test their pages and its contents for conversion efficacy. Their owners create content, upload it on to the live site and forget about it. The way to find the difference between a high-converting page and an inferior page or pages, is split testing.

## Split Testing.

With split testing, you run two or three different designs of the same page against each other, sending customers randomly to the various pages in the test and tracking the results. When a winning page becomes evident, you discard the losing pages and keep the winner. You then create a copy of the winner and start the split testing again by substituting a single element such as a headline, image, price and measuring the new results.

You then keep refining various elements of the page to increase response, conver-sions or even triple sales. When split testing, you only test one element of a page at a time and therefore it can take a while to get a sure-fire winner. There is a faster way...

## Multivariate Testing.

This method of testing overcomes the time problem in split testing, by testing multiple variables on the same page at the same time. All this is tracked by multivariate testing software. Anything from headlines, images, guarantees, phone number placement, security logos, prices, can be tested simultaneously.

### Start By Testing These Pages:
- Home Page
- Product Pages
- Contact Us
- Checkout Pages
- Order Confirmation Page

### Elements On a Page to Test:
- Headlines and Sub headlines
- Product Descriptions
- Call to Action (Most Wanted Response)
- Images
- Design Elements (colors, navigation, logo, tagline, phone number)
- Text Blocks in Specific Areas of Site
- Price
- Button Color & Wording (Read More, Add to Cart, Checkout, etc.)
- Guarantees
- Using the Words *Create Account* or Disguising Account Set up Form
- Forms
- Privacy

## Google Website Optimizer.

Integrating the Google Website Optimizer with your website enables you to test your ideas, with real and actual mathematical results. Implementing optimized pages increases the value of your traffic without increasing your marketing budget.

- Learn more about Google Website Optimizer: www.google.com/websiteoptimizer

# Newsletters.

If and when a visitor leaves your website, as a minimum you want them to have signed up to your newsletter or subscribed to your RSS feed or even clicked an Adsense link making you money on the *'exit click'*. Having them place an order is obviously the goal, but with only .07 in every 100 visitors buying, we have a large number of visitors where we still need to capture their email address before they leave. Once we have the email address we can communicate with them often and offer advice, information, videos and then products.

To get people to opt-in to your email newsletter you can give incentives like a discount code (money off voucher), a free report, how-to guide or even a free video. When you have built a rapport with them, offer them products.

## Opt-In Form.

The opt-in form is normally positioned in the left or right hand column, in the footer or on a specific page, such as the contact and order confirmation page. It can also be presented in a Pop-Up or Pop-Under box that appears when your site visitor enters or exits your website.

*Email Newsletter Opt-In Box Example In Footer of Website*

A pop-up box appears on top of your open window and a pop-under box or advert appears underneath their open window.

I like to test these on an e-commerce store and place the opt-in form in the left or right column, on the order confirmation page and I like to test it on *'Exit'* not entry. When a visitor is leaving your website, this is the ideal time to hit them with a pop-up box with a compelling headline and incentive. The customer is already leaving so you have nothing to lose at this point. However, this needs testing, as some pop-up software can be a bit aggressive and even ugly.

## Example Opt-In Box Text for an E-commerce Website Selling Guitars:

Wait! Grab a free discount code now, good for 10% off any product in the *GuitarsOnline* store. Plus, we'll send you a free exclusive report *'Learn to play the guitar like a pro!'* FREE in the next 60 seconds.

# Blog Marketing.

If you are wondering what this has to do with marketing your e-commerce business, then it is very simple. It creates lots of SEO friendly content!

Google constantly searches for and recognizes new content. Blogs especially are regarded as fresh and relevant content that Google likes to supply to its Google searchers. Google ranks blogs rapidly and high in its search engine results. This is why I recommend you write and post blogs so often.

When you have written and published your blogs on your live site, the 'Ping Option' within the back-end admin of your blog will inform the blog search engines such as Technorati.com, that a new blog has been published, and this is great for SEO.

## Blog Frequency.

Daily or weekly blogs are important because they establish you as an expert in your product category, market or niche and from this valuable information frequency, you can build a loyal following.

Let's be realistic. There will be lots of existing companies in your category or market already promoting the same products as you, so what will set you apart? You must establish yourself as an expert if you want to gain credibility over your competition. For example if you are selling guitar products this may already be a competitive market...

The best thing you can do for your site is to write a keyword-rich blog on a daily basis (where possible) about guitars and the guitar industry. This does not mean you already have to be an expert, but you must position yourself as an expert in this industry, and write captivating and useful content, educating your readers and inspiring your audience to want to buy from you.

Suppose your market is the wine market, and you've been blogging about different types of wine. Consequently, if anyone in any country on the planet is typing into the Google search box *'what is the difference between red and white wine'* your blog stands a great chance of coming up at the top of the search results. People may read your blog, but the goal is to subtly, and swiftly transfer them from your blog to your products so they can purchase wine and wine products from you! This strategy works well repeatedly.

Every time you write and post a blog, another page is added to your website page total, ultimately giving you more weight in the eyes of Google. From an SEO perspective, the more pages you have on a website, the better.

The truth is you need to do everything you can to add control and influence to your website—and one of the main resources in doing so is in creating your own blog.

You can use these same blog topics to submit articles to the directories we previously discussed, further establishing yourself as an expert, drawing more traffic through content, and even gaining links back to your website. But make sure the content is unique.

***Alarming Blog Statistic:***

Of the more than 130 million blogs active since 2002—when blogging started—it's estimated that over 90% are now dormant. This just reinforces the need to promote your blog for the search engines and add fresh new content often (three blogs a week or even daily where possible).

# On-Site Articles.

On-Site Articles are different to the SEO articles mentioned above. On-site articles are of higher quality. As a rule they are 500–800 words or longer and are designed to rank well in Google as well as being written for your on-site visitors to read. Topics covered are buyer's guides, how-to and technical articles, all written with persuasion to sell your products while optimized to rank high in Google. You can link to your on-site article directory from your site footer, customer support pages or a promotional block in your site template.

# Video Marketing.

Video is an excellent medium for you to give your name and your face visibility as an expert in your marketplace and to convert browsers in to buyers.

***Video Ideas:***

1) You can produce product sales videos, product demo videos, product review videos, customer product review videos, technical product videos and testimonial videos

2) Create a YouTube account and host your videos there. Make them shorter than 10 minutes as YouTube has a file size limit. You can then grab the YouTube code, unique for each video you submit and embed this code on to your website page. Also convert to FLV for a smaller file size

3) You can submit any number of videos directly to YouTube , Google Video, or other video sites, within your niche market that will give prospects the opportunity to get to know you. Studies have shown that people respond well to video because more of the five senses are being used in comparison to reading text. Also, as a merchant you can quickly build trust with face to face contact

If you do use landing pages (or opt-in squeeze pages) in your e-commerce marketing strategy you can also use your voice or video to help people emotionally connect to you, your website and your products directly on the landing pages. Then at the end of the video tell them to opt-in to your email list, click to a specific page on your site or even forward the video to a specific product page.

185

4) You can run a series of videos in the form of tutorials or informational videos on your products. People are constantly looking for information online, so if you are providing something relevant and up to date, then they will find you and make their way to your website

# Social Media Marketing.

Social Marketing is the latest medium of online marketing and taps into a networking effect that follows the viral or word of mouth marketing model. Social Media sites are frequented by millions of daily users, and, love them or hate them, you have at your disposal a massive, connected audience.

Social sites including Facebook, Twitter, Google+ and Myspace connect '*friends*' where they can share information, text, photos and social events. Each member creates an account and builds their own network of friends.

## Network Effect.

The idea behind Facebook, Google+ and the other social sites it to get millions of people connected, all sharing information to the benefit of each individual user. The more people they can connect with, the more other people will want to join and the system becomes self-sustaining and self-fulfilling. The power and value of Facebook increases by the number of friends it connects. This is called the Network Effect.

Cynics would say the model behind Facebook is not exactly to get users sharing information but with the aim of getting as many users as possible into their database, because ultimately the more users Facebook acquires the more marketing potential they have. However let's look at the potential for your business to market to these networks and users.

## How You Can Use Social Media?

To get started, create company accounts on Facebook and Twitter and begin to communicate with potential buyers, but do not sell too early or aggressively in the business relationship.

This is an incredibly important and rapidly growing area of Internet marketing, allowing you to promote yourself in a number of different social arenas. The significant thing to remember about social media marketing is that you must be genuine to make a connection with other social users. People are immune to spam, so there is no way you will stand out in a crowd unless you are offering real and relevant information.

**Facebook** has 2 options. A '*Personal Profile*' where you connect with '*Friends*' and A '*Fan Page*' or '*Business Page*' where you get '*Fans*' following you or '*Like*' you. You can create both if required or just choose one profile.

**Twitter** options. My recommendation is to use a service such as **SocialOomph.com** and link to your Twitter account. From within the admin panel you can set up an automated email so when someone follows you, a pre-written email goes out with a welcome message and an offer such as a free report or link to your website. You have 140 characters max so make your message short and sweet.

Don't set your account to '*auto follow*' anyone that follows you as automated systems follow and then when you follow them, they unfollow you. Find people that you actually want to follow and are interested in their Tweets. Also I uncheck the option to '*unfollow*' anyone that '*unfollows*' me, simply because I may still want to follow someone's Tweets, who cares if they unfollow me.

**Google+** is currently in Beta testing at the time of writing, and it's definitely not one to be ignored. Google is going after Facebook and it will be huge for business.

Some of the best social media and bookmarking sites are **www.Facebook.com www. Twitter.com Google+ (https://plus.google.com) and www.MySpace.com**

### *There Are Other Social Media Websites Including:*
- www.Bebo.com
- www.Digg.com
- www.Flickr.com
- www.LinkedIn.com (Professional Networking Site)
- www.Reddit.com
- www.Scribd.com
- www.StumbleUpon.com
- www.Technorati.com
- Read more about Social Media Marketing below in '*Back-End Marketing*'

# E-commerce Shopping Directories.

Shopping Directories and Comparison Shopping Websites have millions of products, thousands of merchants and millions of impartial product reviews. They can help consumers to make informed choices, and as a result, drive higher visitor-to-sales conversion rates on e-commerce websites. They can, if marketed right—again watching the numbers—offer value to merchants.

As e-commerce evolves, sellers and buyers are becoming increasingly sophisticated and adventurous, demanding more choice. Consumers want the widest range of products and stores to compare prices and products, along with the information and data necessary to navigate and view those products efficiently. Merchants can get immediate exposure to the ever-expanding, global population of online shoppers through Shopping Directories.

- http://dir.yahoo.com (Yahoo Directory)
- www.Bestoftheweb.com
- www.Dealtime.com
- www.Kelkoo.com
- www.Dmoz.com (Open Directory Project)
- www.PriceGrabber.com
- www.Shopping.com
- www.Shopzilla.com

# Affiliate Marketing.

Affiliate Marketing is a simple concept. You offer *affiliates* the opportunity to promote your products online, and they earn a set commission for every customer they send to your website who buys from you. The sale must be completed in order to register as an affiliate sale. This can be a percentage or set amount of the sale value.

The affiliate's sales are all tracked using affiliate software that assigns a unique code to every individual affiliate who signs up to promote your affiliate program. You (the merchant) are also assigned a unique code that you install—hidden in the code—on your order confirmation page.

To register an affiliate sale, a customer will click from the affiliate's website or advert and their unique code will be assigned to this customer's path via cookies and tracked through to the checkout confirmation page on your merchant website, where the affiliate's code meets with your merchant code and a sale is completed.

Think of an affiliate as being an independent sales rep. They do not get a salary; they simply make commissions on any sales they send you.

**Pros:** You can get an army of affiliates and websites promoting your products. Plus you can potentially generate many incoming links '*back links*' that we know are essential for Off-Site SEO.

**Cons:** You may get lots of competitors and competing sites that can affect your dominance and profits if you pay the affiliates a little too-well.

*It Is Important to Run the Numbers to Ensure There Is Enough Profit for You to:*

a) Pay the affiliates their commission

b) Pay the affiliate network (if you use an affiliate network company to handle your account)

c) Take some money yourself from each sale

You can choose to stipulate various conditions in your affiliate terms such as '*affiliates must not use PPC ads to promote your affiliate program.*' You would enforce this if you want to dominate the PPC space for your product. You can also determine the cookie length that is assigned to a prospect's tracking and registering as an affiliate sale, meaning they have a limited time to place the order once they have clicked your affiliate's link to your website. The average cookie length is 30 days.

### *The Flexibility of the Program Depends On Whether You Use Your Own Software, or Go Through a Recognized Affiliate Network Such As:*

- www.AffiliateFuture.co.uk
- www.AffiliateWindow.com
- www.Buy.at
- www.CJ.com
- www.ClickBooth.com
- www.ClixGalore.com
- www.LinkShare.com
- www.PaidOnResults.com
- www.ShareASale.com
- www.WebGains.com

# Back-End Marketing

Back-end strategies are marketing methods for generating sales of additional products to an existing customer database or email list. Back-end marketing is critically important for long-term business growth and for the overall success of an e-commerce sales and marketing strategy online.

Back-end marketing is very inexpensive when compared to front-end acquisition marketing as the people you are marketing to are already your customers and you have their details. The largest investment of money was already made in acquiring that customer on the front-end. Remember Lifetime Value?

A key advantage to back-end marketing is that your response rates and conversions will be much higher because your customers already know, respect and trust you.

Despite the benefits of back-end marketing—low cost, higher conversions, higher profits—it's the most underused and even ignored form of marketing strategy.

## Email Newsletter.

One of the best ways to stay in contact with your new and existing customers and sell more products is via a newsletter. This is critical for your e-commerce business success as it keeps your customer informed about new products, new services, and special offers and just keeps you in touch with them in general.

*When a customer gives you their email address having placed an order, they have legally opted in to receive any mailings from you. However, you must have an 'Unsubscribe' link in any emails you send to them so they can opt-out if they wish.*

Your newsletter e-mails can literally be about anything, but they should always give value. Word them in a way to leave your customer wanting more, but do not sell aggressively from day one. Of course, they should also relate to your products and market...

If you are selling guitars online and you have a database of customers who have bought guitars, then you may want to add related guitar accessories or music products or even give away guitar tips and techniques via email or a free PDF report. This concept will entice your customers to learn more, to trust you, and to purchase more products when you offer them.

## RSS.

RSS (Real Simple Syndication) is a way of delivering information from your website to your prospects via an RSS Reader, which displays your content on their PC, Mac, Phone, Laptop, Tablet, Slate or PDA in an easy to view way.

Just like the newsletter strategy above, it is about building and maintaining relationships with your customers and offering valuable information, special offer deals and related products.

An RSS can be applied to your blog posts, blog comments, site content, podcasts, best sellers page and new arrivals page. The idea is that when you add new content it is automatically sent to your RSS subscribers' reader delivering fresh new content.

There is an option to synchronize your blog and newsletter in some of the big name email newsletter software, so that when you post a blog it emails your newsletter list alerting them to the new blog.

# Personalization.

Personalization creates customer loyalty, builds trust and solidifies the relationship between your business and your customer. More importantly, it increases sales.

## Recommendation Systems.

Recommendation Engines or Recommendation Systems find customer patterns by studying your past purchase history and making predications and recommendations based on this data. Essentially as a merchant, they allow you to redecorate your store (website) for each individual customer, based on their buying preferences. This would be impossible for a physical store.

Using Amazon.com as an example, they tailor their website product recommendations and e-mails to their customers. These recommendations appear everywhere across the site, from the home page to product pages, and even on the order confirmation page. As these recommendations are based exactly on your customers' buying history, more sales will obviously result. Do the same and watch as your sales and profits explode.

## Finding Products.

Recommendation systems are critical because they help customers find products they want, whereas on large e-commerce websites they may never find products deep within product categories.

Your customers want to know what you have to offer and what benefits you have for them. You have heard the saying '*what's in it for me*', so give them what they want. Give them recommendations, display related items in their product search results and push related products on product pages, in emails and all across the website when they are logged into their account and viewing your site. These can be as simple as *"You May Also Like"* or *"Recommended For You"*.

Once you have this specific customer data, you can laser target and match your products to your customers' buying wants and desires, so they SPEND like crazy with you.

### Areas of the Website That Can Be Personalized:

- *'Related Products'* block, *'You May Also Like'* block, *'You Might Also Be Interested In'* block, *'Recommended For You'* block
- Frequently Bought Together
- Home Page
- Products Pages
- Best Sellers or Top Selling Products
- New Products or New Arrivals
- Order Confirmation page
- Emails

## Email Personalization.

By personalizing contact you make with your customer you not only build a relationship and trust, but you also increase your sales. Emailing and offering products based on your customers' historical buying data will laser focus your products and sales strategy.

# Social Media.

Creating accounts on the top social sites such as Facebook, Google+ and Twitter allows you to communicate to your existing customers regularly and in real time, keeping your friends and followers in the loop. You simply post comments on Facebook, Google+ and tweet on Twitter about anything related to your everyday business events, new offers and processes, subtly giving links to other interesting and related things, but never taking your eye off the goal of building relationships to sell.

## Feedback Loops.

Facebook pioneered status updates (known as Live Feeds or News Feeds) on the internet, which deliver content and information directly to your friends and followers in real time. Users no longer have to go looking for your information and product updates: they are delivered automatically. As soon as you post content, all of your connections (or friends) instantly receive this information, allowing them to live life in a constant loop. Facebook and Twitter applies this constant action and reaction to friendship and in your case to your business.

Real time updating and not necessarily the number of friends or followers you have, is the key for maximizing business relationships. This model of constant status updates has now been used by many social sites including Twitter.

Twitter's online loop model is an imitation of Facebook but makes it simpler, yet it can be a more powerful model for marketing for some. Tweets are simple, fast and instant.

- Use condensed links in your tweets from *www.tinyurl.com*
- Or from *http://bit.ly/*

**Social Comments & Tweets Could Be Anything Such As:**

- 'New Stock of 42 plasma TVs with free HDMI cable, just arrived'
- 'Unboxing of 200 iPad devices in progress, boy do they look good'
- 'Panasonic Home Cinema Systems uploaded to website - Get FREE Delivery'
- 'On way to CES show in Las Vegas to do deals on new DVD players'
- 'Uploaded New Arrivals to website, many with 30% discounts'
- 'Testing new home cinema system that links your PC music with your TV'

All of the above tweets can be followed by a link to the product or subject you are discussing and are designed to intrigue and excite your followers into wanting the product you are hinting at.

# Existing Customer Loyalty Discount Code.

When dispatching orders to new customers, try enclosing a loyalty discount code of 10%, 20% or whatever your gross profit margin allows. This can be by email message or included in the box with the customer's orders. Use a business card-size card to promote this or an A5 paper flyer.

You can put an expiry date on the code to push your customers to order again by a certain date or leave it open. The coupon code number itself could be *'Discount10'* or *'Loyalty10'* but use your imagination to make the code number itself sound appealing. WhiteStuff.com in the UK do this very well. Using this strategy can increase orders rapidly and by up to 40% and all for the price of a free email or paper insert.

# Congratulations... This Is the End of E-commerce Get It Right!

You now have the ammunition to set up your own e-commerce website and business (or transform your struggling website) and dominate your chosen products, product category, market or niche in rapid time. Get your website live, learn as you grow, market aggressively, keep testing and refining conversions using actual user data and sell on the back-end... Job Done!

- Please give me your feedback (positive or negative) or get in touch with any e-commerce questions you may have: info@ecommercegetitright.com

- And stay connected at my new blog: **www.IanDaniel.com**

- Learn how to squeeze even more profits from your e-commerce store and business: **www.EcommerceJuice.com**

- And look out for my other books coming soon at **www.Amazon.com** on the subjects of: *Advanced E-commerce & Conversion, Web Business, Web Marketing, SEO (Search Engine Optimization) and Buying and Selling Websites.*

## Below You'll Find:

- Thanks
- Further Reading
- Tools & Resources
- Glossary

# Thanks for the Site References.

- **Parking Dynamics:** Home of the Revolutionary No Drill. No Holes. No Damage. 100% *'Invisible when fitted'* Car Parking Sensor. www.ParkingDynamics.co.uk | www.ParkingDynamics.com

- **TGStore:** Worldwide shipping of the biggest Gore bike and running clothing range available online. www.TGStore.eu

- **InCarNetwork:** For everything from Dension iPod Car Kits to leading brand Car Stereos and In-Car Entertainment products. www.InCar-Network.com

- **InCariPod:** Seamlessly connect your iPod to your car radio and take your music with you on the move. www.InCariPod.com

- **Amazon.com:** Launched in 1995 and arguably the best and most successful e-commerce website on the planet. Find everything from Books, CD's, DVD's,

Video Games, and Electronics to Sports Equipment. www.Amazon.com

- **iHerb.com:** For fifteen years, iHerb has striven to supply the best selection of brand name natural products and supplements. www.iHerb.com

- **FatFace.com:** Is a leading designer of men's clothing, women's clothing and kids clothing for an active lifestyle. www.FatFace.com

- **WhiteStuff.com:** Unique and stylish men's and women's clothing for your beach and urban lifestyle. www.whitestuff.com

---

**Please Note:** I have since sold the websites used as examples in this book I once owned. Please do not contact the current website owners regarding e-commerce; Email me with any questions at: info@ecommercegetitright.com

---

# Further Reading.

More of my sites where you can get free and exclusive info, sign up to my newsletters and follow my blogs.

- **www.IanDaniel.com**

- **www.EcommerceJuice.com**

- **www.EcommerceGetItRight.com**

***Book Coming Soon:*** *Advanced E-commerce Conversion Techniques*

## Recommended Books:

There are hundreds of good books and resources on Business, Marketing and Internet Marketing; here are a few of my favorites:

- **How to Out-Sell, Out-Market, Out-Promote, Out-Advertise Everyone Else You Compete Against... Before They Even Knew What Hit Them.** Paul Gorman. ISBN: 0-9549-2060-0

- **Mind Control Marketing** – Mark Joyner

- **The Irresistible Offer** – Mark Joyner

- **4 –Hour WorkWeek** – Tim Ferris

- **The Dip** – Seth Godin

- **Google Power Tools Bible** – Ted Coombs, Roderico DeLeon

# Tools & Resources

## Planning, Mapping Software:

- Microsoft Word: www.Microsoft.com
- Evernote: www.EverNote.com
- Microsoft Visio: www.Microsoft.com
- OpenOffice: www.OpenOffice.org
- MindJet MindManager: www.MindJet.com

## Domain Name Resellers:

- Go Daddy – www.GoDaddy.com (US, global customers and good for .com's)
- 123 Reg – www.123-reg.co.uk (UK Customers)

## Competitor, Keyword, Product Research Tools:

- Wordtracker: www.Wordtracker.com
- Google Adwords Research Tool:
  https://adwords.google.com/select/KeywordToolExternal
- Copernic: www.Copernic.com/en/products/tracker/index.html

## Product Supplier Tools:

- World Wide Brands: www.WorldWideBrands.com

## E-commerce Software:

- osCommerce: www.osCommerce.com
- Magento: www.MagentoCommerce.com
- Etaila: www.Etaila.com

## Blogging Software:

- WordPress: www.WordPress.org and www.WordPress.com

## Courier, Shipping & Logistics Companies.

- DHL: www.dhl.com
- Fedex: www.fedex.com
- Interparcel: www.interparcel.com (The world's top couriers in one place at the most competitive prices)
- Post Office.com: www.postoffice.com (Postal Services in each country)
- Royal Mail: www.royalmail.com (UK Postal Service)

- UPS: www.ups.com
- USPS: www.usps.com (US Postal Service)

## Merchant Account Providers:

- Google Checkout: www.GoogleCheckout.com
- PayPal: www.PayPal.com
- WorldPay: www.Worldpay.com
- SagePay: www.SagePay.com
- Streamline: www.Streamline.com
- MasterCard SecureCode: www.mastercard.com/securecode
- VerifiedByVisa: www.visa.com/verifiedbyvisa
- The 3$^{rd}$ Man: www.the3rdman.co.uk

## Security Accreditations:

- BBB: www.BBB.org (US)
- FSB: www.FSB.org.uk (UK)
- McAfee Secure Code: www.McafeeSecure.com
- Internet Shopping Is Safe: www.IMRG.org/idis (UK)
- Internet Delivery Is Safe: www.IMRG.org/idis (UK)
- Comodo: www.Comodo.com
- Trusted Shops: www.TrustedShops.com

## SSL Certificate:

- GEO Trust: www.GeoTrust.com

## Customer Support & Community Support Software:

- Kayako: www.Kayako.com (paid)
- eTicket: www.eTicketSupport.com Open source (free)
- GetSatisfaction: www.GetSatisfaction.com

## Live Chat Software:

- Live Person: http://solutions.liveperson.com/live-chat
- PHP Live: www.PHPLiveSupport.com

## Email Marketing Software:

- Aweber: www.Aweber.com
- Get Response: www.GetResponse.com
- iContact: www.iContact.com

## Freelance (Outsource):

- Elance: www.Elance.com
- Freelancer: www.Freelancer.com
- ODesk: www.odesk.com

## Article Directories:

- Ezine: www.EzineArticles.com
- Amazines: www.Amazines.com
- Article Bliss: www.ArticleBliss.com
- Ezine Mark: www.EzineMark.com
- Article City: www.ArticleCity.com
- Article Dashboard: www.ArticleDashboard.com
- iSnare: www.iSnare.com
- Go Articles: www.GoArticles.com
- Idea Marketers: www.IdeaMarketers.com
- UPublish: www.Upublish.info

## Shopping Directories:

- Yahoo Directory: http://dir.yahoo.com
- Best Of The Web: www.Bestoftheweb.com
- Deal Time: www.Dealtime.com
- Kelkoo: www.Kelkoo.com
- Open Directory Project: www.Dmoz.com
- Price Grabber: www.PriceGrabber.com
- Shopping.com: www.Shopping.com
- ShopZilla: www.Shopzilla.com

## Social Media Sites:

- Bebo: www.Bebo.com
- Digg: www.Digg.com
- Facebook: www.Facebook.com
- Flickr: www.Flickr.com
- Google+: https://plus.google.com
- LinkedIn: www.LinkedIn.com (Professional Networking Site)
- MySpace: www.MySpace.com
- Reddit: www.Reddit.com

- Scribd: www.Scribd.com

- StumbleUpon: www.StumbleUpon.com

- Technorati: www.Technorati.com

- Twitter: www.Twitter.com

## Social Media Tools:

- Social Oomph: www.SocialOomph.com

## Affiliate Networks:

- Affiliate Future: www.AffiliateFuture.co.uk

- Affiliate Window: www.AffiliateWindow.com

- Buy.at: www.Buy.at

- Commission Junction: www.CJ.com

- Click Booth: www.ClickBooth.com

- Cix Galore: www.ClixGalore.com

- Link Share: www.LinkShare.com

- Paid On Results: www.PaidOnResults.com

- Share A Sale: www.ShareASale.com

- Web Gains: www.WebGains.com

## Google Tools:

- Google+: https://plus.google.com (Share on the web, like sharing in real life)

- Google Accounts: www.google.com/accounts (Keeps all Google Services in 1 Account)

- Google Add URL (.com): www.google.com/addurl (Submit Your New Website to Google's Global Index)

- Google Add URL (.co.uk): www.google.co.uk/addurl (Submit Your New Website to Google's UK & Global Index)

- Google Alerts: www.google.com/alerts (Keep Up to Date with Your Competitors or Market)

- Google Analytics: www.google.com/analytics (Site Analytics, Data & Performance Reporting)

- Google Apps: www.google.com/apps (Multiple Apps all in 1 Place)

- Google Adsense: www.google.com/adsense (Post Adwords on Your Website)

- Google Adwords: www.adwords.google.com (Pay Per Click Advertising)

- Google Adwords Client Center: www.google.com/adwords/MyClientCenter (Handle Multiple Adwords Accounts)
- Google Adwords Editor: www.google.com/adwordseditor (Manage Adwords Campaigns)
- Google Buzz: www.google.com/buzz (Share updates, photos, videos and more)
- Google Checkout: www.googlecheckout.com (Google's Checkout Service)
- Google Commerce Search: www.google.com/commercesearch (Optimize Product Search)
- Google Docs: www.docs.google.com (Create and edit web-based documents and spreadsheets)
- Google Global Market Finder: http://www.google.com/adwords/globaladvertiser/marketfinder.html (Find new markets overseas)
- Google Insights: www.google.com/insights/search/# (See what the world is searching for)
- Google Mail: www.gmail.com (Server Based Email Client)
- Google Merchant Center: www.google.com/merchants (Upload Your Product Data)
- Google Places: www.google.com/local/add (list local your business and get top rankings)
- Google Product Search: www.google.com/products (Product Comparison Site)
- Google Translate: http://translate.google.com/translate_tools (Translate Your Website)
- Google Trends: www.google.com/trends (Reflects what keywords people are searching for on a daily basis)
- Google Webmaster Tools: www.google.com/webmasters/tools (Improve Website Data)
- Google Website Optimizer: www.google.com/websiteoptimizer (Split & Multivariate Testing)

# Glossary

- **3G:** Refers to the third generation of developments in wireless technology, especially mobile communications. Offers voice, data and rapid data internet transfer.

- **Affiliate:** In Internet marketing, an affiliate is a person or company that sends visitors to a website in exchange for commissions, per visit or per sale.

- **API (Application Programming Interface):** An application programming interface (API) is an interface implemented by a software program to enable interaction with other software, much in the same way that a user interface facilitates interaction between humans and computers.

- **Article Marketing:** A method of promoting your website by writing articles and submitting them to article directories. These articles will be distributed and published online, and they allow you to include a resource box to link back to your website. This has the potential to enhance the credibility of the business and drive traffic to the website via back links.

- **Back-End:** This means marketing to customers once they have ordered from you. Back-end is before once they are customers and front-end is marketing to them as prospects before they become customers.

- **Bandwidth:** The rate of data that can be transmitted by bits per second through a channel on your computer and referenced when downloading and uploading data.

- **Blog:** Short for *'Web Log'*. A website or area of a website often used as an online diary, but can be used for so much more when marketing an e-commerce website. Posting blogs consistently generates fresh content, which is appealing to Google and to your site visitors. Readers can leave interactive comments on the blog for each post.

- **Bluetooth:** *Bluetooth* technology allows electronic devices to communicate wirelessly over short distances (using short length radio waves) from fixed and mobile devices, creating *'personal area networks'* (PANs).

- **Bounce Rate:** is a key online measurement expressed as a percentage of visitors who only see a single page on a web site before leaving. So they enter and leave on the same page without clicking to another page.

- **Broadband:** Is a fast and permanent internet connection. Commonly 10-100 times faster than dial-up internet. Domestic broadband connections will be between 3–5 MB (Mega Bytes) per second.

- **Call-to-Action:** Also known as Most Wanted Response. This is your intended action for your website visitor. What do you want them to do when they land on your website? Opt in to an email list, buy a product, complete a survey?

- **Canonicalization:** rel="canonical" is the Canonical Attribute. In web search and search engine optimization (SEO), URL canonicalization deals with web content that has more than one possible URL. Having multiple URLs for the same web content can cause problems for search engines - canonicalization determines which URL should be shown in search results. Use the attribute on pages required.

- **CMS (Content Management System):** The engine of an e-commerce website, it's the back-end admin organized and structured for you the retailer to manage products, process orders, customer area and to display content and products in an organized fashion on the website for the user to interactively purchase products, etc.

- **Conversion:** A desired user action on your website be it a sale, an email opt-in, a contact or completion of a survey.

- **CRM (Customer Relationship Management):** Technology used to manage a company's customer interaction and sales. Software is used to synchronize these processes, especially those in customer service, technical support, and marketing. These processes can be streamlined to attract new customers and maintain customer loyalty by reducing marketing costs overall.

- **Cross-Sell:** Cross-selling is a very simple sales technique online or offline. Simply selling additional products to your customer that they may be interested in, such as items related to their previous purchases.

- **CSS (Cascading Style Sheets):** A language of style sheets used for web pages written in HTML. It offers flexibility when organizing and updating the colors, layouts, and fonts on a website across multiple pages in one go. Prevents the need to make changes on multiple pages.

- **Discount Code:** Also known as voucher codes, these give you the option to run promotions and offer your customers a discount off your products when they place an order on your website.

- **Drop-Shipping:** To send a product from your supplier direct to your customer without you handling the product. This is usually done covertly so your customer believes you have shipped the product.

- **Downtime:** When your hosting service temporarily fails due to a technical glitch and your website goes offline for a certain time. It needs to be corrected immediately to keep your website up and running.

- **E-commerce:** Electronic Commerce. The process of online business transactions and selling from a website. Also known as electronic marketing for the purpose of buying and selling products or services online to retail or business consumers.

- **Email Newsletter:** A way of building a relationship and keeping in touch with your customers and prospects by writing and sending regular emails using email-marketing software, which manages the customers and emails for easy automation. You market to your subscribers by giving advice, information and products.

- **Exit Strategy:** An *Exit Strategy* is a strategic decision made when you start your business to withdraw from your business generally by selling.

- **Exit Click:** When a visitor leaves your website. By displaying and using Adsense advertisements on your site, you can make money when people leave or click off.

- **Flash:** Flash was formerly called *"Macromedia Flash"*, but has now been relabeled as "Adobe Flash" since Adobe purchased Macromedia software in 2005. Flash is streaming animation for web pages. Sometimes Flash is a portion of an html web page, and sometimes a web page is made entirely of Flash. Either way, Flash files are called *"Flash movies"*. These are special .swf format files that stream to your web browser screen as you watch them.

- **Firewall:** A security system that helps protect a computer from malicious attacks coming in from the internet.

- **Front-End:** This means marketing to prospects before they buy from you and become customers. Front-end is before they are customers and back-end is marketing to them once they have become customers.

- **Fulfillment:** Is when you outsource an area of your order process from taking orders to delivery of products to customers. Fulfillment houses are companies that can handle everything for you from manufacturer to delivery. This allows you to concentrate on marketing your business.

- **Google:** This is the most popular search engine available, and it attracts 80% of the search volume online. Ranks websites based on a mathematical algorithm but delivers very accurate results. When you focus on SEO this is the search engine to focus your efforts on.

- **Gray Imports:** A gray import is the genuine product, but sourced from a foreign market where prices are typically a lot cheaper and sometimes specifications are slightly different. The biggest issue with *'true'* gray imports (and not knock off clones or replicas) is the manufacturer's warranty and whether this is honored. Gray Market items are predominantly sold on the internet or through wholesale channels where it is difficult for the buyer to properly inspect the product prior to buying. The internet is a hot spot for gray imports and replica products.

- **Gross Profit:** Calculated as sales minus all costs directly related to making and delivering those sales. These costs can include manufacturing expenses, raw materials, labor, selling, marketing, shipping and other expenses.

- **HTML (Hyper Text Markup Language):** is the predominant markup language for web pages. It provides a means to create structured documents by using structural components for text such as headings, paragraphs, lists as well as for links, quotes, and other items.

- **In-House:** This is the use of the company's own money, resources, and staff for their business production of software, web design, customer support, sales and support, as opposed to outsourcing the necessary work to other companies.

- **Java:** A programming system developed by Sun Microsystems and used to produce code and scripts to add various functions to your website.

- **JPG or JPEG:** Pronounced *'Jay-Peg'* and is the most common online graphic image format. This format uses a compression technology that has the ability to reduce part of the data, without the difference being undetectable to the human eye. This allows for size reduction, resulting in smaller data storage, less bandwidth usage and faster load speeds.

- **Landing Pages:** Also known as squeeze pages. These are used as a powerful lead generation tactic, and optimizing these via split testing and multivariate testing can super-charge your profits. The idea is to get traffic into your email loop so you can build a relationship and then offer products.

- **Links (Hyperlinks):** Is a reference to a web document that the reader can directly follow, or that is followed automatically. Links join webpages to make websites and link websites together to make the World Wide Web.

- **Logistics:** The process of shipping and delivering goods. From collection at the website company to delivery with your customer.

- **Meta Tags:** Meta tags are HTML codes that are inserted into the header on a web page, after the title tag. These essentially tell the search engines about your website and more specifically the page the tag is on. Top tags are Page Title, Meta Description and keywords.

- **Most Wanted Response (MWR):** Also known as Call to Action. When a visitor lands on your website, what do you want them to do? Buy a product, opt in to your email newsletter, call a number?

- **Multi-Channel Retailing:** Selling online and offline and synchronizing the two methods.

- **MP3:** Where JPEG is compressed images, MP3 is the sound equivalent; compressed music and audio files. A data format that clips the sound at either end of the audible ranges to reduce its size.

- **Multivariate Testing:** This method of testing overcomes the time problem in split testing, by testing multiple variables on the same page at the same time. All this is tracked by multivariate testing software. Anything from headlines, images, guarantees, phone number placement, security logos, etc., can be tested simultaneously.

- **Net Profit:** Often referred to as the bottom line, net profit is calculated by subtracting a company's total expenses from total revenue, thus showing what the company has earned (or lost) in a given period of time (usually one year). Also called net income or net earnings.

- **No Follow Attribute:** rel="Nofollow" attribute provides a way for webmasters to tell search engines "Don't follow links on this page" or "Don't follow this specific link." Following a link means Google passes PageRank and anchor text. This is used on non-important pages such as privacy, help, terms and conditions.

- **Off-Site SEO (off-page SEO):** Using SEO strategies external to your website to boost rankings in Google, including but not limited to: link building, article marketing, link reputation, link popularity.

- **On-Site SEO (on-page SEO):** Using SEO strategies within your website to boost rankings in Google, including but not limited to: page titles, header tags, internal linking, PageRank distribution, use of the 'no follow' tag and more.

- **Operations (Order Management):** The fulfillment of customer orders from sale to shipping, which includes handling returns and supporting orders and warranties backed by customer support.

- **Outsource:** The process of contracting work to another company or individual frequently at a lower cost. Many businesses use outsourcing to save money instead of hiring employees, and it can often be used for anything from web design to writing content.

- **PageRank:** Google PageRank (Google PR) is one of the methods Google uses to determine a page's relevance or importance. Important pages receive a higher PageRank and are more likely to appear at the top of the search results. Google PageRank (PR) is a measure from 0-10. Google Pagerank is based on backlinks. The more quality backlinks the higher google pagerank. Improving your Google page rank (building quality backlinks) is very important if you want to improve your search engine rankings.

- **Pay On Results (POR):** An agreement with a service provider that stipulates (you the customer) only pays for the service provided when the pre-agreed results and targets are achieved. Great for Search Engine Optimization (SEO).

- **Pay Per Click (PPC):** A form of advertising where you place an advert or product on a website and tailor this to fit your target market. When the advert is clicked by a potential customer to go to your website the advertiser pays money. For example, Google Adwords are PPC ads.

- **Personalization:** Tailoring your website, marketing and specifics to fit your customers' needs exactly based on their user data. For example, when you have data of the type of products your customer orders, you can focus those products in their emails and on their homepage when they log into their account on your website.

- **Recommendation Engine (Recommendation Systems):** Integrated software systems on your website that collate actual customer buying data allowing you to personalize and match your products to your customers' buying interests and behaviors, and tailor your marketing to each specific customer.

- **RSS (Real Simple Syndication):** RSS is a format for delivering regularly changing web content. Many news-related sites, weblogs and other online publishers syndicate their content as an RSS Feed to whoever wants it.

- **SEM (Search Engine Marketing):** This is a type of Internet marketing promoting websites so they become more visible through search engine results. Popular SEM vendors are Google AdWords and Yahoo Search Marketing.

- **SEO (Search Engine Optimization):** SEO is used to increase traffic to your website by generating higher search results in Google and the other main search engines Yahoo and Bing. This is a 2 step process of On-Site SEO (on-page) and Off-Site SEO (off-page). When working optimally in synergy, this is extremely powerful for rankings and consequently your sales and profits.

- **Shipping:** The process of delivering goods, from your business to your customer.

- **Site-Wide:** Across the whole website.

- **Skype:** A provider of internet based voice communications. With *Skype* you can make free calls over the internet to other people on *Skype* for as long as you like, to wherever you like. It is free to download. Using VOIP (Voice Over Internet Protocol) as a method to carry voice calls over the main telecommunication networks.

- **Social Media:** A type of medium and website relying upon user interactivity and participation where the content is generated by users. Bookmarking is a major component where users share information. Popular social media sites include Facebook, Google+, Twitter, Digg, and Reddit. Customer product reviews and blog comments can be considered social networking elements.

- **Split Testing:** Is the process of running two or three different designs of the same page against each other, to test and track the results. When a winning page becomes evident, you discard the losing pages, create a copy of the winner, substitute a single element such as a headline or image and measure the results. You then keep refining various single elements of the page to increase response, conversions or even triple sales.

- **Title Tag:** Commonly known as the Page Title, it's the main text that describes an individual page online. It is the single most important on-page SEO element (behind overall content) and appears in three key places: Top of Browser, Search Result in search engine and External Websites when displaying your site.

- **Traffic:** Visitors to your website. It can be measured daily, weekly, monthly or annually and the more traffic you get the more sales you can expect.

- **Turnover:** Turnover is the volume of business over a period of time. If a company is selling goods, then stock turnover is also the number of times that their inventory of goods is sold over a given period.

- **Up-Sell:** Up-sell is a marketing term for suggesting higher priced products or services to a customer who is considering a purchase.

- **Uptime:** Opposite to Downtime and a measurement of the reliability of your hosting and its ability to keep your website live online.

- **Usability (Web Usability):** Is an approach to make websites easy to use for your customers, prospects and visitors, without requiring them to undergo any specialized training. It is about making your website intuitive so it makes sense to everyone.

- **UGC (User Generated Content):** Content on a website contributed solely by visitors to your website. This includes customer product reviews and write-ups, blog comments, forum posts, social media content, online communities.

- **URL (Uniform Resource Locator):** A website addresses starting with *'www'*.

- **W3C (World Wide Web Consortium):** An international standards organization for the World Wide Web headed by Tim Berners-Lee. It is made up of different organizations that work to maintain the standards of the Internet, and it currently has over 300 members.

- **Web 2.0:** A term used to describe modern web applications that work through informational sharing. Some examples of these are online communities, web applications, social media websites, video sharing websites, hosting services, blogs, and wikis. These all involve users changing the content of the website by being interactive with the information provided.

- **Wikipedia:** (Pronounced wik-i-pee-dee-a) is a free, web-based, collaborative, multilingual, free-content encyclopedia project that anyone can edit and contribute to.

- **Word of Mouth (WOM):** The most powerful form of advertising available and it's free. Simply a recommendation from one person to another about your product, service or business. Run your business with the right values and Word of Mouth will add massively to your bottom-line profits.